IMAGES
of America

NORTH BALTIMORE AND ITS NEIGHBORS

IMAGES
of America

NORTH BALTIMORE AND ITS NEIGHBORS

Thomas W. Boltz

ARCADIA
PUBLISHING

Published by Arcadia Publishing
Charleston SC, Chicago IL, Portsmouth NH, San Francisco CA

Library of Congress Control Number: 2009923287

For all general information contact Arcadia Publishing at:
Telephone 843-853-2070
Fax 843-853-0044
E-mail sales@arcadiapublishing.com
For customer service and orders:
Toll-Free 1-888-313-2665

Visit us on the Internet at www.arcadiapublishing.com

CONTENTS

ACKNOWLEDGMENTS

The majority of images in this book appear courtesy of the North Baltimore Area Historical Society (NBAHS) and the Wood County Historical Society (WCHS). Others were obtained from private collections that are identified at the end of each caption.

I would like to thank the NBAHS for access to its archives. Society president Pam Lang Seiler and members Janice Emahiser and Phyllis Everly Mercer merit special recognition for helping preserve the society's collection. I am also grateful to the staff of the WCHS, especially curator Randy Brown, who facilitated my research of the museum's archives. Further, Tom Konecny, Hancock-Wood Electric Co-op public relations director, was especially helpful in gaining permission for me to use pictures from his company's archives.

Many people generously contributed photographs from their private collections and helped identify people and places pictured. These included Sam Bretz, Millie Kramp Broka, Beth Wall Brumbaugh, Nancy Buchanan, Iris Sewell Holloway, Maxine Dulaney Hudson, Bonnie Knaggs, James R. Kramp, Paula Rockwell Miklovic, Dr. William H. Roberts, Ken Searfoss, Beverly Woessner Straley, Marge Featheringill Waterfield, and Wilbur Wirt Jr.

During my research, I was fortunate to be able to consult several individuals who possess extensive knowledge of Wood County's history. Bonnie Knaggs, North Baltimore's official town historian, was an incomparable and unstinting source of information. A past president and founder of the NBAHS, Knaggs was instrumental in establishing the society's historical photograph collection and has donated many pictures from her personal collection to the archives. Knaggs has been photographing the North Baltimore area since the 1940s, and several of her photographs are used in this book. Retired Ohio State extension agent Richard Martin was especially helpful on southern Wood County's agricultural history. Nancy Brumbaugh, a native Jackson Township resident and a retired educator, provided information on southern Wood County's one-room schools.

Finally, I wish to thank my wife, Jean, for reading and editing my manuscript and providing many insightful comments. Without her support, writing this book would have been a much more difficult task.

INTRODUCTION

The northern border of northwestern Ohio's Wood County is delineated by the Maumee River along whose banks are found Fort Meigs and old river towns with a rich, well-recorded history. In contrast, southern Wood County provides few hints of its once dynamic and occasionally colorful past. Its communities also have stories of marching armies, struggling pioneers, and, most notably, the unrestrained exploitation of oil deposits that gave rise to wide-open boomtowns and sudden wealth. This book attempts to recall and preserve that history.

Southern Wood County was among the last areas of Ohio to be settled, and it remained very sparsely populated until the 1850s. This was due largely to its location at the southern edge of Ohio's Great Black Swamp, an area covered by dense forests of towering oak, ash, and hickory coupled with wet swampy ground that made travel nearly impossible. Native Americans had long shunned the area except for hunting or taking refuge from enemies in times of war. They settled instead either to the south of the swamp or 25 miles to the north along the Maumee River. White settlers followed a similar pattern, claiming land to the north and south in the very early 1800s but leaving the swampy area unpopulated.

During the War of 1812, Gen. William Hull marched his army through the Black Swamp on his way to Detroit. This was the first visit by large numbers of European Americans to the area. Hull's 2,500-man force spent two days traversing the area and camped for one night on the low ridge where North Baltimore is now located. His army cut a road through the forest as they slowly moved north toward the Maumee River and on to Detroit. After the war, this road served as the major route between Findlay and the settlements along the Maumee River to the north that became Perrysburg and Toledo.

It was not until the 1830s that the eight swampy townships in southern Wood County began to be claimed, drained, and settled to a significant extent. The area that became Liberty Township had its first settlers in 1825, while Henry Township's first pioneer, Henry Shaw, purchased his land in 1829. The first settlers arrived in Perry Township in 1831 and in Montgomery Township in 1832. Bloom, Portage, and Milton Townships saw their first settlers in 1833. Jackson was the last to be settled beginning in 1839 and remained the least populated township in Wood County in the 19th century.

The Black Swamp proved to be excellent farmland when drained. The southern Wood County area is characterized by an extremely flat terrain except for an east-west sand ridge along the county's southern border. An approximately one-mile-long elevated north-south limestone ridge runs through part of Henry Township, and lower limestone ridges and sand hills are found throughout the region. When settlement increased, towns and homes tended to be located on

7

these relatively high spots, while the rich, fertile lowland was used for crops. As forests were cleared, logs were used to build settlers' cabins, and saw and barrel stave mills were established.

The coming of the railroads in the 1870s provided a major economic boost to the area. The Baltimore and Ohio Railroad (B&O) built its main east-west line from Baltimore to Chicago through Perry, Bloom, Henry, and Jackson Townships. There was intense rivalry among the communities for the locations of depots, which would lead to the growth of some villages and the demise of others. By the 1890s, the region was further served in north-south directions by the Cincinnati, Hamilton, and Dayton and the Toledo and Ohio Central railroads. In 1902, the Toledo, Bowling Green, and Southern Electric Interurban Line was built through the region, giving local residents transportation to most of Ohio's major cities.

While the railroads brought growth, the oil boom of the late 1800s spurred the period of greatest prosperity for the region. Wood County was in the heart of the Lima-Trenton Oil Field, and the first of hundreds of wells was drilled in 1886 near North Baltimore. Huge quantities of oil and natural gas were extracted from the area over the next decade. Farmers grew rich from leasing their land to drilling companies, and oil company owners and investors became extremely wealthy. However, poor conservation practices and unregulated exploitation of the oil field led to its early demise. The oil boom was over by 1915, although a few wells were still pumping in the 1950s, and a handful of wells remained in operation as of 2008.

Over the years, many small hamlets grew and declined as their viability was affected by the railroads and later by the oil boom. The pioneer community of Woodbury, which once had a post office, a store, and several log cabins, disappeared by the mid-1800s. Denver declined when a hoped-for railway depot was located just to the east in North Baltimore. Others, such as Bays and Trombley, came into existence to provide goods and services to the oil field workers and their families. Once the oil ceased to flow, their customers moved on, their stores closed, and their citizens moved away. Today the sites of most of these towns have become farmland, with little or no evidence that they were once thriving communities. A few houses remain on the sites of other small communities, but these hamlets remain anonymous, lacking even a road sign recording the community's historical name.

After the oil boom ended, the economy and population of southern Wood County stagnated. Towns like North Baltimore, Cygnet, and Hoytville continued as local market centers and homes to small factories, and most retained healthy commercial main streets for the next five decades. However, the pace of change was slow, and growth was all but nonexistent. In the early 1960s, small-town commerce began a steady decline when Interstate 75 facilitated travel to larger shopping centers and chain stores. By 1980, the towns of southern Wood County had become largely residential communities with few, if any, commercial stores.

The photographs in this book show details of community activities, farming, and family life, and events such as fires that were previously recorded primarily in newspaper articles. Many of these images have not been previously published. Descendents of early settlers and families who came during the oil boom kindly made many of their private photographs available to the author. Others are new acquisitions of the Wood County Historical Society and Museum and the North Baltimore Area Historical Society. Together these photographs record the area's lively but nearly forgotten past.

One

CLEARING THE
BLACK SWAMP

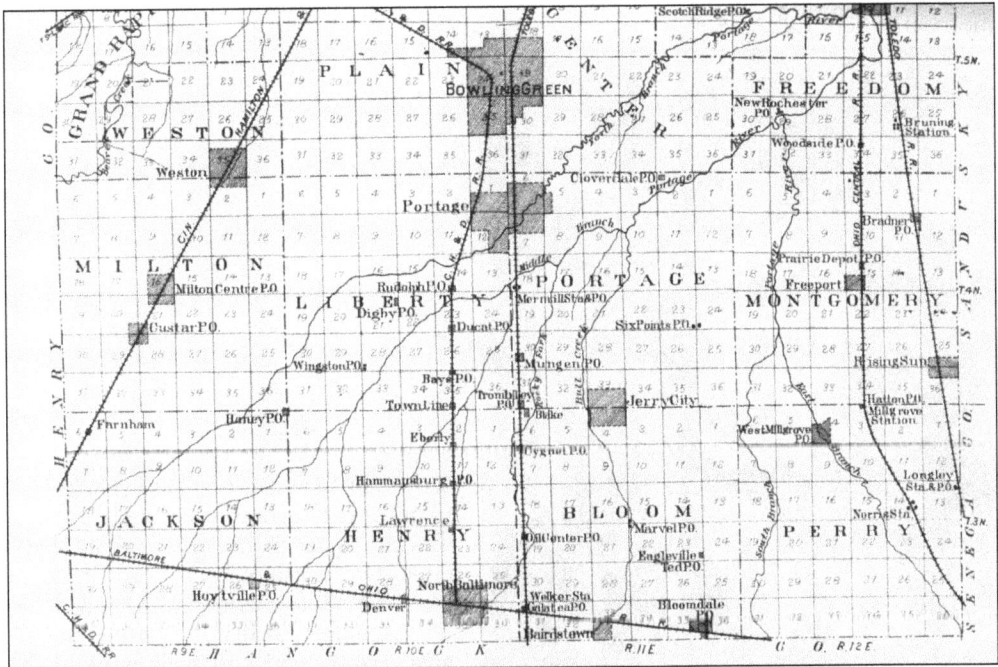

Prior to 1800, Wood County, Ohio, was covered by the desolate, unpopulated Black Swamp. By the end of the 19th century as shown on this 1897 map, southern Wood County was completely settled. Many of the towns shown on the map, such as North Baltimore, still existed in 2008. Others, such as Bays, have all but disappeared. (J. H. Beers and Co. 1897 *Historical and Biographical Record of Wood County, Ohio.*)

This early 1900 picture is the earliest known photograph of Rocky Ford Creek (originally called Portage Creek). In the 1830s, the first pioneers in what was to become Henry Township settled on the high ground north of the creek. John Beeson built a water-powered gristmill along its banks in 1834 in what was later to become North Baltimore. The mill was greatly welcomed by the local settlers. (NBAHS.)

Originally from Connecticut, Charles Grant (1809–1896) was one of Henry Township's first pioneers, settling in 1832 on 40 acres north of Rocky Ford Creek. He and his wife, Susan Hassinger, had seven children. In 1835, he planted the area's first orchard with seeds provided by John Chapman, known in American folklore as "Johnny Appleseed." In 1836, Grant was elected the township's first constable for law enforcement. (Author's collection.)

Early Henry Township pioneers built this log cabin on what is today two miles west of North Baltimore on Quarry Road. The first settlers began to clear the land for crops in the 1830s. The first home sites were located along the limestone ridge upon which North Baltimore's Main Street is located today. The cabin was torn down in the mid-1920s. (Author's collection.)

In the 19th century, the Black Swamp's huge trees were a major timber source, and local farmers frequently worked in the lumber industry during the winter months. Horses were used to move logs to the mills, usually during winter when the frozen ground supported heavy loads. By the early 1900s, most of the large trees had been harvested, and the remnants of the original forests were surrounded by farmland. (NBAHS.)

In the mid-19th century, Wood County sawmills like the one pictured here were thriving. Road improvements and railroad construction in the 1870s encouraged establishment of additional mills to provide lumber to eastern and local markets. Also, more reliable and efficient steam engines powered the mills, which increased productivity. Both logs and cut lumber were shipped by rail to Lake Erie ports, Baltimore, and other east coast cities. (NBAHS.)

Wooden barrels were widely used for shipping and storage during the 19th century, creating a demand for barrel staves, such as those being produced in this photograph. By the 1870s, clearing efforts had begun to deplete the number of large trees in Wood County. As a result, many of the area's stave mills moved to Michigan. (Beth Wall Brumbaugh.)

As soon as they could afford to do so, many settlers replaced their log cabins with clapboard houses. These were easier to build, could be designed in a variety of floor plans, and reflected the advance of civilization into the wilderness areas. However, such houses were more expensive, and some people continued to live in log cabins until the early 20th century. (NBAHS.)

Bassett L. Peters is considered the founder of North Baltimore. In the 1850s at what was known as Peters Crossroads, he ran a general store, served as justice of the peace, sold real estate, established the first church and newspaper, and was the town's first mayor. When the B&O built its main line through the area in 1873, Peters settlement was selected for the local depot. (NBAHS.)

George D. Chase was a rival of Bassett Peters in the development of Henry Township. A Union Army veteran, Chase settled on a farm just west of North Baltimore in 1866, began a lumber business, and founded the hamlet of Denver, hoping in vain that a rail depot would be located there. This photograph shows George, his wife, Mary Caskey Chase, and their youngest son, Clyde. (Author's collection.)

This 1884 winter photograph is the earliest known picture of North Baltimore. Looking south from the intersection of Broadway and North Main Streets, the photograph shows the original area of Peters Crossroads. The streets were unpaved, and most buildings were still constructed of wood. Briefly known as New Baltimore, the name was changed to North Baltimore to prevent confusion in the mails with another New Baltimore in Ohio. (NBAHS.)

14

Two

NORTH BALTIMORE AND THE OIL BOOM

In this photograph, three carriages carrying women and children appear to be stopped at an oil well site, a somewhat dangerous location for visitors. The northwest Ohio oil boom of 1884 to 1915 brought great prosperity to North Baltimore, where a well was first drilled in 1886. Only about 40 percent of the field's crude oil was extracted primarily because operators did not preserve necessary natural gas pressure. (Dr. William H. Roberts.)

Highly explosive nitroglycerin was used to fracture rock in the final drilling stages or to improve the flow of oil in older wells. Metal tubes, called torpedoes, were filled with liquid nitroglycerin and dropped into the wells by skilled "shooters." Wagons like the one above were used to transport the nitroglycerin from an explosive company's magazines to the well sites over rough dirt roads. Accidents were frequent and deadly. (WCHS.)

An oil well site, such as the one in this photograph, usually consisted of a wooden derrick with pulleys and rope to hoist the drill bits and casing pipe, a stationary steam engine, and a series of belts and wheels to transmit power from the engine to the drill or pump. Wells were drilled by speculators as well as by established oil companies. (Dr. William H. Roberts.)

This picture of North Main Street was taken shortly before the great fire of 1891. Built in 1890, the town hall with its tower can be seen on the left. The First National Bank with its conical roof is on the right. Henry's Opera House is the ninth building on the left side. The fire began behind the brick building on the far left, which housed a saloon. (NBAHS.)

This is an 1891 bird's-eye view of the northwestern quarter of North Baltimore. The smoke is from an oil tank fire. Oil wells were drilled in most sections of town, including along Tarr Street where many of the towns most prosperous citizens resided. The brick buildings on the right lined Main Street's west side. In the foreground, an eastbound freight train is passing through town. (NBAHS.)

17

TIME TABLE
Baltimore & Ohio R. R.
November 10th, 1889.

WEST BOUND.

LEAVE	A M	P M	P M	A M	P M
Pittsburg	.....	‡6 30	‡7 30	‡5 45	.....
Wheeling	‡7 10	9 05	10 05	8 30	‡2 40
		A M	A M		
Zanesville	10 10	12 01	1 25	11 47	5 57
	P M			P M	
Newark	12 30	2 25	2 25	1 10	6 15
	A M	P M		A M	
Columbus	†7 20	11 05	†2 20	11 20	†4 30
		A M		P M	
Mt. Vernon	‡11 38	1 32	4 33	2 11	‡7 41
	P M				
Mansfield	12 40	2 36	4 55	3 33	8 42
Tiffin	2 25	4 04	8 03	†5 27	10 20
Fostoria	2 43	4 23	8 30	5 55	10 45
Nth. Balto.	.....	.....	8 55	7 19	.....
Deshler	3 22	5 03	9 22	6 46	11 40
Defiance	4 05	5 43	10 13	7 30	A M
Auburn Jc.	.....	6 40	11 34	8 30	2 07
			P M		
Milford Jc.	.....	7 47	1 15	.....	.....
Ar Chic'go	9 40	10 55	5 15	.....	.....

EAST BOUND.

LEAVE	A M	P M	A M	P M	P M.
Chicago	*10 10	*2 55	†8 10	.....	*5 05
	P M	P M	A M	A M	
Auburn June	.....	7 05	1 38	†4 07	9 36
Deshler	3 45	8 35	4 15	6 23	11 16
				P M	A M
N. Balto..	.....		3 45	5 55	11 56
Fostoria	4 25	9 17	5 23	7 19	12 04
Tiffin	4 43	9 38	5 55	7 46	12 29
	A M				
Columbus	.....	.....	.....	.....	.....
		A M	A M	P M	A M
Newark	8 05	12 55	12 10	12 40	*4 10
					P M
Wheeling	10 50	6 25	4 00	5 10	‡7 00
ARRIVE AT Pittsburg	.....	9 50	6 45	00	.....
	A M	P M	P M	A M	P M
Washington	11 45	4 05	6 50	7 10	8 51
Baltimore	12 45	5 15	7 50	8 20	10 00
Philadelphia	3 15	7 20	10 30	11 00	.....

‡Trains run daily. †Daily except Sunday.
*Daily except Monday. Sleeping and dining cars on all through trains.

W.W. PEABODY,   C.O. SCULL,
Gen. Man., Chicago.   Gen. Pass. Agt. Balto. Md.

In the late 1800s and early 1900s, the railroads were enormously important to southern Wood County residents, effectively serving as their main link to the outside world. According to this 1889 B&O train schedule, two westbound and three eastbound passenger trains stopped daily at the local depot, which was located in a prime site on South Main Street in the center of town. By the mid-1890s, the Cincinnati, Hamilton, and Dayton Railroad also served North Baltimore with northbound travel from its East Broadway station, a less desirable location. In addition, residents could travel north and south on the Toledo and Ohio Central Railroad from Galatea, a village located one mile east of North Baltimore. The station agent filled an essential role. He manned the depot, advised travelers on rail connections, sold tickets, arranged freight shipments, and operated the telegraph. Usually only one or two agents were assigned to depots in small towns. (NBAHS.)

ROCKWELL'S FLOURING MILLS, NORTH BALTIMORE, OHIO.

Rockwell's Flourmill was among the town's first industries. Built in 1873, George Rockwell purchased the business in 1880. Wheat cleaners began the refining process in the basement; first-floor rollers processed the wheat into course flour; second-floor purifying and bolting reels refined the flour; and a third-floor flour sifter completed the process. A stationary steam engine powered the mill. (NBAHS.)

The North Baltimore Bottle Glass Works, located in the northwest section of town, was one of three glass companies that built factories in the town to take advantage of cheap local natural gas to fire their glass furnaces. The 56 workers in the photograph included many young boys who assisted the skilled adult glassblowers. When the local gas supplies ran out, the companies left town. (WCHS.)

North Baltimore's town hall, located at 205 North Main Street, was a source of civic pride. The first floor housed the local fire companies, the police station, and jail. The second floor contained the town clerk's office and the council chambers. A fire bell in the left tower was rung to summon volunteer fireman, while the right tower contained pulleys to hoist the canvas fire hoses for drying. (NBAHS.)

After much political discord, North Baltimore issued a franchise to build a water purification plant and distribution system in June 1891. Unfortunately the system was not completed at the time of the great fire in October. This brick building on East High Street contained the water pumps, purification equipment, and a stationary steam engine. The tall standpipe held water to increase water pressure. A 1906 fire destroyed this building. (NBAHS.)

50000   Water Works, North Baltimore, O.

Frank P. Clark served as mayor of North Baltimore during the great fire of 1891. A successful merchant who wanted to please local businessmen, he was reluctant to crack down on saloons and other illegal activities. However, during his term, North Baltimore began to build a water purification plant and install water mains throughout the city. (NBAHS.)

Mayor Clark owned a successful drug store and sold furniture on the second floor of his building at 117 North Main Street. In this picture, Clark is standing in the center of the store's doorway. He may have been having a sale on roll top desks since two are displayed on the sidewalk. (NBAHS.)

In this view, Frank P. Clark is standing in the aisle of his drug store. The containers on the shelves hold pharmaceutical ingredients. In the 19th century, druggists often compounded prescriptions individually. The display cases contain cigars, magazines, school supplies, and other products for sale. The store was destroyed in the great fire of 1891 but was quickly rebuilt and back in business within several months. (NBAHS.)

Although he was not the original owner, Clark lived at 305 South Tarr Street in one of the largest brick houses in North Baltimore. In the 1890s, Tarr Street was the first village street to be paved. Lined with tall trees, South Tarr Street was considered the most beautiful street in town and was home to many of the wealthiest and most influential citizens. (NBAHS.)

In 1891, the Bechtel family operated a saloon in a wooden building at 104 North Main Street on the east side of the street. Bechtel and Sons was destroyed in the great fire but subsequently was rebuilt near the same location in a more substantial brick building. Horace Bechtel is the mustachioed man standing in the doorway. The three young men typify the rough characters that frequented these establishments. (NBAHS.)

During the oil boom, North Baltimore had 23 saloons, including Charley Pifher's, shown here. Most were in cheap wooden buildings and were sparsely furnished with a carved wooden bar, spittoons, and a few tables. Patrons were usually single and were often rowdy and drunken oil workers who sought entertainment especially on payday weekends. Pifher's dog in the chair is the only creature known to have died in the great fire. (NBAHS.)

Frank Orwig was one of the colorful individuals attracted to North Baltimore during the oil boom. A snappy dresser who wore a gold watch and carried a silver-handled cane, he owned a profitable saloon on the east side of North Main Street. Orwig left town after his saloon was destroyed in the great fire. He died under mysterious circumstances in Bucyrus in 1892. (Marge Featheringill Waterfield.)

Erected in 1888 at 125 North Main Street, the two-story Chalfont building was one of the town's most attractive commercial buildings. A men's clothing store with large plate-glass windows occupied the first floor. Housing offices, the ornate second-floor facade contained stained-glass windows behind a carved stone balcony. The facade's roofline was ornately decorated reflecting the architectural tastes of the Victorian era. It burned in the 1891 fire. (NBAHS.)

At 10:00 p.m. on October 30, the great fire of 1891 began behind a North Main Street saloon. A strong southwesterly wind quickly spread the flames, which destroyed 49 structures. The Fostoria Fire Department aided the local firemen in stopping the fire by using the high walls of the opera house and the First National Bank as barriers. This picture shows the devastation that awaited the town the next morning. (NBAHS.)

This c. 1900 bird's-eye view looks northward from the top of the old South School building at 124 South Second Street. Property owners had totally rebuilt all of Main Street destroyed in the great fire of 1891, usually with new brick construction. The Henry Electric Power Plant's two brick and metal smoke stacks are on the center right of the picture, and North Main Street is just beyond them. (NBAHS.)

John and George Deter operated a grocery store at 124 South Main Street from the 1890s until the early 1900s. The store occupied one half of the International Order of Odd Fellows (IOFF) Block, which was located at 124 South Main Street. In this picture, a local fraternal organization, possibly the IOFF, has assembled for a group picture with each member wearing their lodge regalia. (Bonnie Knaggs.)

In this interior photograph of Deter Brothers grocery, clerk Jay Northrup (on left) is helping a customer. On the right, co-owner John is holding his account book while talking to another patron. The store's products were displayed in glass cases or stocked on shelves behind the counters. Customers gave their orders to the clerks who then located the items and bagged them after payment. (NBAHS.)

Bicycle riding was a popular sport for both sexes in 1890s North Baltimore. There were several bicycle clubs in town that sponsored excursions as well as organized racing competitions. The *Weekly Beacon*, a local North Baltimore newspaper, often carried articles about Fred Rockwell, a local champion bicycle racer who was the son of George Rockwell, the flour mill owner. (NBAHS.)

Here six fashionably dressed North Baltimore women are enjoying an evening card game in a well-furnished Victorian room lit by electric light. A cut-glass dish filled with apples sits upon the wooden table. During the oil boom, many of North Baltimore's businessmen built fine homes, and their families were able to enjoy luxury goods and leisure time that had not been available to earlier generations. (NBAHS.)

During the Civil War, 30 Henry Township men enlisted in the Union Army; 18 died in service. In 1881, 14 area veterans formed Sill Post No. 57 of the Grand Army of the Republic. The membership posed for this picture in the late 1890s when most were in their 50s or older. The local post was both a social club and a political and patriotic organization. (Author's collection.)

In 1895, the Ohio National Guard established a unit in North Baltimore designated as Company K, 2nd Infantry Regiment. The unit was mobilized in April 1898 for duty with the U.S. Army in the Spanish-American War. However, the war ended before the unit had completed training. In this picture, the unit is mustered in front of a building at the corner of West Walnut and North Main Streets. (NBAHS.)

Three

QUIET VILLAGE LIFE

This *c.* 1905 photograph of a quiet, deserted North Main Street was probably taken on a Sunday or a holiday. By then, North Baltimore was becoming a relatively tranquil village. When oil production rapidly fell after 1901, the economy also declined. The town's population fell from a high of 3,500 in the 1890s to approximately 2,500 in 1920. Small factories remained, but merchants increasingly relied on farmers for customers. (NBAHS.)

Beginning in 1902, the Toledo, Bowling Green, and Southern Electric Interurban Line provided North Baltimore residents with an alternative to the steam railroads for north-south travel. An adult round-trip fare to Toledo was $3. Before the company built a station at 137 South Main Street, passengers boarded the cars in the middle of North Main Street, often blocking traffic when two cars arrived simultaneously. (NBAHS.)

This print shop is typical of those found in small towns. North Baltimore supported two newspapers in the early 1900s, the *Weekly Beacon* owned by George W. Wilkinson and the *Times* owned by Clarence L. Huddle. Here Huddle is operating a small hand-fed press used for printing small products. Part of the much larger newspaper press can be seen in the lower right corner. (NBAHS.)

Many North Baltimore merchants operated several different businesses simultaneously. William Diebley operated both the livery stable (in the photograph above) and a mortuary. Most funerals were still held in home parlors or in local churches, but transportation and burial were handled by Diebley. He maintained a stable of beautiful white and black horses to pull the funeral hearses and carriages like those in the photograph below. Because antibiotics would not come into use for another 30 years, children frequently died from infectious diseases. Diebly owned several white hearses for children's funerals, which were pulled by white horses. Both white and black horses were used for adult hearses and for the mourners' black carriages. Diebly's livery stable also boarded horses and rented horses and carriages. The stable, torn down in the 1980s, was located at 226 North Main Street. (NBAHS.)

Diebly's hearses and matching teams were used for the Neely family funeral in December 1902. Grace Neely and her three children were tragically killed when their horse bolted and dragged their carriage into the path of an oncoming train. The father was watching from a nearby field. In the picture, the white hearses are carrying the children's caskets down North Main Street on the way to Maplewood Cemetery. (NBAHS.)

Henry's Opera House at 129–133 North Main Street, the town's primary location for entertainment, is shown here in December 1902. The 1,000-seat opera house was on the third floor with access through the double doors in the center of the building. The first floor contained two stores while the second floor housed professional offices. (NBAHS.)

"BIBI"

A Dream of a Night.

—Given By—

Timoleon Temple,

No. 67

RATHBONE SISTERS.

Henry's Opera House

North Baltimore

Oct. 8 and 9, 1903.

This Henry's Opera House program was for a play given by the local temple of the Rathbone Sisters, the female auxiliary of the Knights of Pythias, a national fraternal organization. The opera house was used for a variety of activities including school graduations, lectures, political meetings, vaudeville, and theatrical performances. Touring companies frequently performed in North Baltimore, including John Phillip Sousa and his band. Ticket prices were relatively inexpensive, and the opera house was a popular source of entertainment for oil workers. Albert G. Henry, a physician and one of North Baltimore's leading entrepreneurs, consecutively built three opera houses on the same site. Each was destroyed by fire in 1888, 1894, and 1911, respectively. He had sold the last opera house prior to the 1911 fire. The new owners decided not to rebuild because they were facing increasing competition from the town's two new motion picture theaters. Dr. Henry was also a drug store merchant, builder, and operator of the town's electric power plant. (NBAHS.)

Main St. looking North. North Baltimore, Ohio.

This c. 1910 view of North Main Street shows a well-maintained brick street with nearly every building occupied. The Toledo, Bowling Green, and Southern Interurban tracks are in the center, while the B&O's double tracks cross them in the foreground. Miller's Restaurant was located on the east side of the street just north of the railroad. There has been a restaurant on this site for over 100 years. (NBAHS.)

In this c. 1910 interior view of Miller's Restaurant, Emil Miller and his young son Paul are standing on the right near the windows. The waiters and the customer are unidentified. The day's specials, which included oyster soup for 25¢ and an oyster and ham dinner for $3.25, are posted over the counter. (NBAHS.)

34

In 1910, Barbary M. Eiting's millinery business, located at 110 South Main Street, catered to fashionable women in North Baltimore. In these photographs, big hats with bows and feathers, characteristic of the period, are displayed in the front window (above) and the interior (below) of the store. Eiting's business is an example of the many fine stores that thrived in North Baltimore during the oil boom. According to an 1898 business directory, the town had three jewelry stores, three millinery stores, three dressmakers, three men's tailors, two shoemakers, two photographers, six confectionery stores, and one piano and organ store. Wealthier residents also made shopping trips to larger cities such as Toledo or annual excursions to Chicago or New York to purchase fine goods. (NBAHS.)

In the early 1900s, Horace Bechtel (on the right in the photograph to the left), who had previously operated a saloon, opened the Manhattan Pool Hall at 104 North Main Street. Many considered pool halls places of vice, and the town had its share of pool sharks and gamblers whose activities were criticized in *Weekly Beacon* editorials. Six Brunswick tables, pool cue racks, chairs for spectators, and spittoons can be seen in the picture below. Generally working class men patronized local pool halls. However, many of the town's young men of all social classes would occasionally visit to enjoy a game or two. (Left, Bonnie Knaggs; below, NBAHS.)

In this photograph, Charles Way is driving his Flanders car on North Main Street accompanied by Anna Miller and Emil Miller and his wife Mary. Way was a successful insurance agent who could afford an automobile, an item that was beyond the means of most North Baltimore citizens. This Flanders automobile had a right side steering wheel, which was unusual; most American cars were made with the steering wheel on the left. (NBAHS.)

In this early 1900s photograph, North Baltimore's volunteer firemen are ready to depart from the B&O depot for a firemen's convention in a neighboring town. The town band is standing behind them along with a number of citizens gathered to see them off. The local firemen looked forward to these annual conventions with their parades, picnics, and good times away from the potentially disapproving eyes of their fellow citizens. (NBAHS.)

South Main Street had escaped destruction during the great fire of 1891. Consequently it contained a large number of its original 19th century buildings. In this view looking south from the railroad, the Pennsylvania Hotel (later renamed the Baltimore Hotel) on the east side was the oldest hotel in North Baltimore. The town's other hotels during 1900–1920 were the Columbia and the Central. (Sam Bretz.)

In this c. 1905 photograph, interurban car No. 130 is heading north across the B&O track on South Main Street. The three-story corner building housed Hughes Department Store on the ground floor, apartments on the second, and a lodge and ballroom on the third floor. The building in the right background is a grain elevator, built in the 1870s to store grains purchased from area farmers. (NBAHS.)

Clarence W. Ellis, pictured on the business card above, was the proprietor of the Baltimore Hotel, the former Pennsylvania Hotel, which catered to salesmen and others seeking inexpensive accommodations. Incidents at the hotel occasionally made the *Weekly Beacon*'s front page. In addition to barroom fights and a guest's robbery, these included a shooting when a prominent local businessman discovered his wife with another man at the hotel. The European plan meant that meals were not included in the room price. Ellis advertised his hotel's barroom on the back of his business card shown below. The "Huebner brew" was a local beer brewed by the Toledo-Huebner Brewing Company from 1902 until prohibition began in 1919. The building was demolished and replaced by a gas station around 1930. (NBAHS.)

The T. A. Robinson cigar factory, located at 139 South Main Street, manufactured Cannonball and Don Morano brand cigars for the local market. In the 19th and early 20th centuries, local cigar factories were common. When Robinson first opened in the 1890s, the firm employed men but, like most cigar factories, switched to young women, who would work for a much lower wage. The women worked in teams of three—two rollers and a buncher who boxed the finished cigars. The cigar box lid, seen below, advertised Cannonball cigars for 5¢ each. By the 1920s, cigarettes were becoming popular, and demand for cigars fell dramatically. National brands took over more of the remaining cigar market, and T. A. Robinson cigar factory was forced to close. The building was razed in 1989. (Above, Maxine Dulaney Hudson; below, NBAHS.)

Because it did not have any banks and only one major department store, South Main Street was always secondary to North Main Street as a commercial area. South Main Street was also home to more specialized stores such as the Ritter farm machinery dealership. In this early 1900s photograph (above), a new threshing machine parked along the west side of South Main Street has attracted a number of onlookers. Ritter's was also a noted gathering place for area farmers to chat and exchange information. His store was located in a 19th century wooden false-front building, a type which had been erected in large numbers along Main Street as the town was being built. In the 1910 photograph below, South Main Street was visited by the Pacific Borax Company's 20 Mule Team advertising promotion for its borax-based laundry soap. (Above, NBAHS; below, Dr. William H. Roberts.)

North Baltimore's all volunteer fire department was first organized in 1877. By the 1890s, there were two fire companies operating under one fire chief, the Rescue Hook and Ladder Company and the Buckeye Hose Company. The two were combined by 1910. In this *c.* 1905 photograph, the Rescue Hook and Ladder Company members are posing before the town hall. The ladder wagon was pulled by hand. (NBAHS.)

At 1:45 p.m. on May 6, 1906, fire broke out in the Dillinger Block at 103 North Main Street. A strong wind hampered the firemen's efforts, and, although the building was a total loss, the blaze was prevented from spreading. In this photograph, a large crowd has gathered to watch the fire. Many had aided in salvaging goods from the burning building. (Dr. William H. Roberts.)

On March 25, 1907, at 4:30 a.m., the fire bell summoned the North Baltimore Fire Department to the Henry Electric Power Plant at 115 West State Street where an overflowing oil purifier had ignited. Despite the firemen's efforts, the building was destroyed, and the town was without power for months. This picture was taken in the early morning while the fire was still burning. (Dr. William H. Roberts.)

Ruins of the Big Fire, Sept. 9, 1911, North Baltimore, Ohio

On September 9, 1911, North Baltimore suffered its greatest fire since 1891. Most of a block on the west side of Main and south of West Broadway was destroyed including the third Henry's Opera House, Giha's Confectionary, Hoffman's Drug Store, and Stouffer's Hardware. The Hardy Bank building was heavily damaged. Low water pressure, caused by faulty water company equipment, hampered fire-fighting efforts. (Bonnie Knaggs.)

43

Dr. Albert Henry built North Baltimore's electric power plant in 1890. It was never a financial success, and he sold it in 1910. The man in this c. 1910 picture is Abner Boltz, the plant's engineer, and his son Forest Boltz. A gas engine is in the background, a generator is in the right foreground, and the plant's control panel is on the right wall. (Author's collection.)

North Baltimore's oldest manufacturing building, located at 331 East Cherry Street, was first used by the North Baltimore Furniture Company in 1891 and later housed a match factory. Although greatly modified, the building was still being used in 2008 by the D. S. Brown Company, which was the town's oldest operating business. This c. 1900 photograph shows the east side of the building. (NBAHS.)

By 1905, the France Stone Company was one of North Baltimore's major employers. The company employed over 200 seasonal workers by 1915. The building pictured above housed the stone crusher and shifters that were originally powered by coal-fired steam engines. Major customers were the B&O and other railroads, which used the quarried limestone for track bed ballast. The company first used narrow-gauge railroad cars to move stone from the quarry floor to the crusher building but later switched to a much faster conveyor belt. The quarry pictured below was located on the northwest side of town on Mitchell Road. As it expanded, it severed at least one road leading out of town. The crusher building was torn down in January 1971, and quarrying stopped in the 1980s. By 2008, the abandoned quarry had filled with water. (Above, Sam Bretz; below, NBAHS.)

France Stone Co., North Baltimore, Ohio.

It was always a major event when the circus came to town for it brought an atmosphere of excitement and a chance to see the exotic. In the photograph at left, the Wallace Brothers Circus is unloading its animals and equipment from its railroad cars in the center of North Baltimore on the sidings west of the depot. The first event would have been the parade of animals and performers down Main Street on their way to the big top tent on the edge of town. For many people, this was their first look at an elephant, camel, or other unusual animals. In the photograph below, spectators line the street several deep, and all the balconies are filled with onlookers as the parade passes the block between the First National Bank and the Central Hotel. (NBAHS.)

Equally popular in the late 19th and early 20th centuries were Wild West shows, which brought a romanticized picture of the American West to audiences back East. Buffalo Bill Cody originated the western shows, and many imitators followed with shows featuring American Indians on horseback, cowboys roping steers, shooting exhibitions, and battle recreations to excite the audiences. Similar to the circus, the Wild West shows began with a parade down Main Street. Included in the show visiting North Baltimore in the c. 1905 photograph at right is a steam calliope. American Indians in full headdresses were a favorite and thrilling sight since the Indian Wars on the Great Plains were less than 20 years in the past. In the lower photograph, the American Indians are passing the Hardy Bank building on the left, while the parade stretches past city hall to the north. (NBAHS.)

In this *c.* 1905 winter photograph, North Main Street's residential area was unpaved. Although Main Street's commercial areas and Tarr Street were paved with brick in the early 1890s, other areas remained unpaved until a decade or so later. Many were nearly impassable in bad weather. On one occasion, the fire department's pumper became stuck in a mud hole on the way to a fire. (Sam Bretz.)

This home at 213 North Tarr Street was owned by William E. and Jesse Diebly. His livery stable and funeral business provided them a comfortable living in North Baltimore even after the oil boom. The house, built around 1900, was typical of those owned by many small businessmen. Porches were large enough to accommodate the entire family on warm evenings, and lots usually included a stable and other outbuildings. (NBAHS.)

Prior to the 1920s, most village homes used iceboxes instead of electric refrigerators to keep their food cool. Rural homes used ice even later. For a fee, local dealers such as Laney and Company delivered ice by wagon from their icehouse, located beside the railroad between North Main and North Tarr Streets. Deliveries were generally made at least once a week. (NBAHS.)

In a rare view of the backyard of a North Baltimore house, Charles Roberts is surrounded by his pet dogs. The neighbor's clothes can be seen hanging on a line to dry, a nearly universal practice before automated clothes dryers came into use. In the right foreground is a Southside Grocery wagon, which made home deliveries for a fee. Homeowners sometimes kept livestock in backyard stables until the village council prohibited the practice in the early 1900s. (Dr. William H. Roberts.)

In 1905, North Baltimore had two school buildings. The larger south building at 124 South Second Street, shown here, educated both high school and elementary students. A smaller north building at 115 East Cherry Street served elementary grades only. Most rural schools had only one room and served students only through the eighth grade. The high school curriculum offered science and foreign language classes for the few college-bound students. (NBAHS.)

This photograph, taken in either 1903 or 1904, shows the north building elementary school faculty and principal with a group of students watching. In the early 1900s, teaching was one of the few professions open to women. Many of North Baltimore's elementary teachers were women whose families were longtime village residents. Male teachers tended to be concentrated in the high school faculty. (NBAHS.)

50

Most of the 1907 graduating class posed for this photograph. Members included Earl Alworth, Emma Bartz, George Black, Edna Crawford, Ray Donnan, Howard Fitzpatrick, Creole Justice, Edith Mercer, Archie Peifer, Earl Smith, Frank Sterling, Adda Sweet, Haskell Sweet, Kate Wiley, Gerald Wilkinson, and Jennie Wood. Each was required to speak during graduation exercises. The 1906–1907 high school enrollment totaled 111 students, drawn from a village population of approximately 2,500. (NBAHS.)

This c. 1900 photograph was taken at a banquet held by North Baltimore's Free and Accepted Masons, Lodge No. 561. Organized in 1890, the lodge first met in the Hughes block at 110 South Main Street but moved in 1914 to 207 North Main Street. They remained there until that building burned in 1985, forcing a move in 1988 to a new lodge at 165 West High Street. (Author's collection.)

The Woodmen of the World, Columbia Camp No. 17, was established in 1893. Through its national organization, the camp provided insurance to its members, assistance to families of deceased members, and other social and welfare benefits. In this picture, lodge members have assembled for a final tribute at the grave site of Ira F. Naugle. Members are in uniform and carrying axes as part of their ritual. (Sam Bretz.)

The *Weekly Beacon* ran this humorous picture of six North Baltimore bachelors in 1908, which was a leap year. The men are, from left to right, Sam Schoonover, Ben Bower, Arthur French, Joseph H. Stahl, Arthur P. Schmidt, and Charles E. Way. Four of the men are listed in the 1910 federal census as being married. (NBAHS.)

Around 1900, J. C. Thompson formed this boys' band to provide entertainment for local events and a worthwhile activity for the town's young men. Many parents supported the effort as a way to keep their sons busy and away from less desirable places such as the local pool halls. The funds to purchase the instruments were raised by subscription. Thompson is the man standing in the last row. (WCHS.)

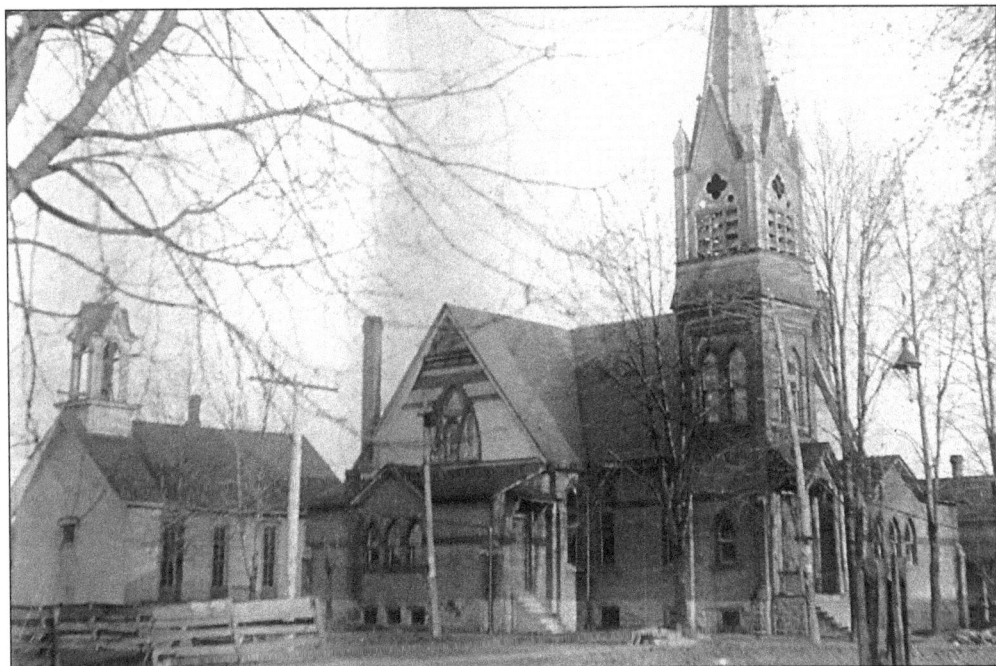

The Methodist Episcopal Church, 201 South Second Street, is the oldest congregation in Henry Township, dating to 1846. It is currently known as St. James United Methodist Church. In 1881, the congregation constructed the white frame building on the left. In 1890, the larger brick church on the right was completed. The smaller church continued to be used for both church and other meetings until it was razed in the early 1900s. (NBAHS.)

In this *c.* 1905 photograph, the United Brethren Church congregation has assembled on a Sunday morning for a group portrait. The church building was constructed in 1910 at 119 West Broadway and was razed in 1959. It was noted for its front stained glass window of the Good Shepherd. The congregation has gone through several mergers and was known as the Church of the Good Shepherd United Methodist in 2008. (NBAHS.)

St. Augustine's Catholic Church, built in 1892 along with the parsonage for $4,000, was located on the southwest corner of Second and Oak Streets. It served a growing congregation until it was destroyed by fire in 1930. The congregation then purchased the old North School at 115 East Cherry Street, which was remodeled and renamed Our Lady of the Miraculous Medal Catholic Church. The old parsonage is still standing. (NBAHS.)

This *c.* 1950 photograph shows the First Presbyterian Church at 117 North Tarr Street. The building was originally constructed by a Church of Christ congregation on South Street. When that congregation disbanded, Presbyterians purchased the building and moved it, in 1892, to its Tarr Street location. It served that denomination until 1999 when the Presbyterian congregation disbanded. In 2008, the building was a Salvation Army facility. (NBAHS.)

When World War I began in 1914, the United States declared itself neutral while Canada joined the Allied Powers. However, many Americans favored the Allied side and joined the Canadian military. William Zorn, a young North Baltimore resident pictured here in his Canadian uniform, enlisted in the Canadian Army in 1915 and served on the Western Front. He was a member of Company C, 10th Battalion, 1st Canadian Division. (NBAHS.)

PROGRAM

Bugle Call—(all rise)
Song—"America" .... Congregation
Prayer.
Responsive Reading—Psalms 46 and 47,
.... Congregation
Duet—"Keep the Home Fires Burning,"
.... Mr. and Mrs. Fausnaugh
Honor Roll is Called
and Service Flag Unfurled
Solo—When the Boys Come Home,"
.... Mrs. Borough
Remarks .... Rev. Hill
Solo...... .... Miss Mabel Robinson
Offertory—Harp Solo..Miss Winifred Radebaugh
Reading .. .. Miss Jeanette Fausnaugh
Quartette...... ....
Mr. and Mrs. Fausnaugh,
Mrs. Borough and Mr. Herbert Baker
Address—"My personal Glimpses of the War,"
.... Mr. William Zorn
Solo .... Miss Evelyn Kalmbach
Song—"Star Spangled Banner,"
.... Primary Class, with Harp
Song—War Hymn (America).... Congregation
"God bless our noble men:
Send them safe home again:
God bless our men.
Keep them victorious,
Patient and chivalrous.
They are so dear to us.
God save our men."
Benediction

North Baltimore's Honor Roll

Daniel Reddin,	Sam Speaker,
Roy Langmade,	Gail Beckett,
O. O. Neddinriep,	Henry Wise,
Carl Bucher,	Roger Wilson,
John House,	Charles Abbott,
Ray Johnson,	Ray Boardman,
Seldon Slane,	Charles Ritter,
Roy Culver,	Lyman Kalmbach,
✓ Harold McGann,	Listen Waters,
Harold Ducat,	Wayne Mason,
William Becker,	Vernon Wymer,
Ray Boltz,	Patrick Wichener,
Romaine Weaver,	Clark Martin.
Clyde Talmage,	Arthur Henning,
Griffith Lathrop,	J. Oberdorf.
Ben Slaughterbeck,	Muriel Copus,
Lawrence McGuire,	Frank Baker,
John Paul Bogle,	Earl Brooks,
Charles Brainard,	Ralph Earlywine,
Earl Jordan,	Ernest Irwin,
Howard Freeman,	Hector Bongero,
Elmer DeRose,	Edgar Chapman,
Elmer Straley,	Tom Swinehart,
Jay Davis,	Charles Wylie,
Howard Todd,	Ross Kuhlman,
Clenis Mercer,	John Willick,
Russel Wrede,	George Carr.
Harry Chapman,	Edward Wrede,
Russel Foley,	Lawrence McCoy.
Warren Rogers,	Howard Wrede.
Leon Waters,	Harry Do[Sol

In 1917, the United States entered World War I, and North Baltimore's citizens enthusiastically supported the effort. However, some reactions were less than admirable, such as when a mob from the local saloons broke into the high school and removed and burned the German language books. As the fighting wore on, more sober patriotic meetings were organized. This program is from a service for the North Baltimore soldiers and sailors in service and for young men about to be conscripted. William Zorn, the main speaker, related his experiences with the Canadian Army to inspire the audience to support the American war effort. At the time, Zorn had returned to North Baltimore after being wounded fighting the Germans on the western front, recuperating in Canada, and being discharged from the Canadian Army. (NBAHS.)

Dr. Charles D. McCormick was a North Baltimore veterinarian who joined the Veterinary Corps of the U.S. Army in 1917. Although trucks were increasingly used, the U.S. Army still maintained thousands of draft horses and mules to pull artillery and transport supplies, and veterinarians were needed to keep them in good health. After the war, Dr. McCormick returned to his practice in North Baltimore. (NBAHS.)

In 1919, conscription was ending, and the U.S. Army was once again recruiting volunteers to fill its enlisted ranks. As part of a nationwide recruiting and public relations campaign, the U.S. Army sent tank demonstration detachments to communities throughout the country. In this photograph, one unit is demonstrating the capabilities of a U.S. Army Renault F-17 tank on the France Stone Quarry's Mitchell Road property before a crowd of spectators. (NBAHS.)

With the war still fresh in everyone's mind, the town's annual Memorial Day parade and services took on renewed meaning and attracted large crowds, as shown in this 1920s-era photograph. Five North Baltimore area men died during World War I while in the military. They were Charles Lawrence, Morris Neiman, John Weaver, Howard Wrede, and Vernon Wymer. (NBAHS.)

At 3:45 p.m. on April 23, 1919, a tornado struck North Baltimore, touching down at the end of West Broadway Street and proceeding in an easterly direction. It caused major damage to the North Main Street commercial district, blowing out windows and destroying brick walls. Houses and barns to the east were destroyed as the storm moved toward Galatea where it dissipated. Surprisingly no major injuries were reported. (NBAHS.)

Four

GOOD TIMES
AND BAD TIMES

North Baltimore's B&O station was still an important place in this 1923 photograph, with four to six passenger trains stopping daily. The two men are Frank Paden Sr. (left), station agent from 1915 to 1937, and Harry Fisher. A baggage cart sits next to an open door leading to the baggage room. The passenger waiting room entrance can be seen on the left. (Author's collection.)

In October 1923, the North Baltimore Commercial Club in conjunction with the B&O Railroad sponsored a three-day Golden Jubilee celebration of the railroad's arrival in the village in 1873. For the occasion, the B&O sent the *Atlantic*, an old 1832 engine, pictured above, and modern freight steam engine No. 4382, pictured below. The exhibition was staged in the center of town near the depot, and thousands of people attended, touring the railroad equipment and taking short rides on cars pulled by the *Atlantic*. A parade was held in which the guest of honor was Frank Swinehart, the engineer of the first train to arrive in the community. Swinehart, age 73 in 1923, recollected that the first station was in Bassett L. Peters's general store and at that time there were only about six houses in town. (NBAHS.)

Initially the Toledo, Bowling Green, and Southern Interurban Streetcar Line competed with the steam railroads for freight and passengers. This interurban freight train is entering town sometime in 1919 or 1920. Later automobiles and trucks proved to be more significant competitors, and the interurban ceased operation in October 1930. Most of the tracks were removed for scrap except on North Main Street where some remain buried in the pavement. (NBAHS.)

Five physicians are listed on this page from a 1920s North Baltimore directory. Health care in the 1920s was in transition due to medical advances and more modern practices. However, doctors still made house calls and listed their home phone numbers in the directory. The nearest hospitals were in Findlay and Toledo, so, except for the most serious problems, doctors treated people locally, and they convalesced at home. (NBAHS.)

PHYSICIANS

E. A. POWELL, M. D.

Res. Phone 125   Office Phone 20

C. S. CAVETT, M. D.

Office and Residence Address, 212 N, Main St.

Phone No. 147

J. R. ARCHER, M. D.

Office Phone 223 R   Res. Phone 98

G. W. & EARL FOLTZ, M. Ds.

PHYSICIANS

DR. G. W. FOLTZ   Office Phone   DR. EARL FOLTZ
Res. Phone 100   **193**   Res. Phone 9

In 1932, Wilbur L. Wirt Sr. started Wirt Motor Sales at 237 North Main Street, pictured above. Wirt originally sold Chrysler's Dodge and Plymouths cars as well as General Motors' Pontiacs and Oldsmobiles. However, General Motors forced him to drop the Chrysler line since Chrysler was a rival company. Business was slow during the depression, and Wirt felt he was doing well to sell three or four cars a month. When World War II began, car manufacturers focused on military orders, and production for the civilian market ceased, forcing Wirt to close until 1946. Below is a 1940 photograph of Wirt's repair facility. The men pictured are, from left to right, Durwood Wilson, Harold McKee, Howard Goldner, Marty Yokum, and an unidentified man. Wirt's dealership continued in business until 1965. (Above, Wilbur Wirt Jr.; below, NBAHS.)

North Baltimore was a major market town for area farmers, not only for the sale of crops but also for purchasing supplies and farm equipment. Worline Winner and his son Ovid Jack Winner purchased Mike Rogers's farm equipment dealership in 1920. The family operated the business until 1983 as the Winner and Son Farm Implement Company, first selling McCormick Deering equipment and later selling Oliver and White equipment. In the above photograph, standing in front of their 128 South Main Street location are, from left to right, Worline Winner, Ovid Jack Winner, Mike Rogers, and an unidentified McCormick company representative. In the interior view below, various farm implements are displayed for sale including a tractor and several farm implements with seats attached that could be pulled by a team of horses. (NBAHS.)

After the repeal of prohibition in 1933, Feese and Steiff Beer Distributorship opened as a Wooden Shoe Beer wholesaler at 115 West State Street. In the above photograph, the owners and employees pose with their trucks. North Baltimore had been a battleground between saloon owners and anti-alcohol activists since the oil boom. While local anti-saloon groups welcomed prohibition in 1919, many other residents purchased bootleg liquor during the 1920s. (NBAHS.)

North Baltimore was hit hard by the Great Depression, as reflected in this late-1930s photograph of empty buildings on East Broadway. Farm prices dropped, northwest Ohio area factories closed, local merchants failed, farms were lost, and most residents had less money to spend. As a result, many owners did not maintain their buildings and allowed them to deteriorate. These buildings once housed a barbershop, laundry, and monument sales. (NBAHS.)

The old Rockwell Mill at the corner of East State and East Streets, then owned by the North Baltimore Grain Company, was destroyed by fire on the morning of July 19, 1930, when sparks from a passing steam locomotive reportedly started the blaze. Although North Baltimore firemen soon arrived on the scene, they could not contain the conflagration. Within 90 minutes, three of the four major buildings were totally destroyed, including the 55-year-old landmark mill. Word soon spread, and large crowds, seen in this photograph, gathered to watch as the flames began to break through the roof. The Cygnet, Hoytville, Jerry City, Bloomdale, and Findlay fire departments aided local firemen, but the heat was so intense that several neighboring houses caught fire, and for a time, the firemen feared that the adjoining Everett Lumber Company would also be lost. The *Weekly Beacon* reported that several firefighters were burned or otherwise injured as a result of the blaze. (Paula Rockwell Miklovic.)

The Old N.B. H.S. Jan 28 1926.

In the late evening of January 28, 1926, the south school burned, and North Baltimore lost one of its oldest buildings and a source of community pride. The school was built in two sections, the first in 1884 and the second in 1903. A witness reported that when the first engine arrived, flames were already sweeping up through the stairwell of the old section. The wood floors had recently been waxed, a factor that may have contributed to the fire's rapid spread. Despite the local fire department's best efforts to stop the blaze, the building was soon reduced to the total ruin seen in this picture. The 1903 section is on the left, and the 1884 section is on the right. Student and faculty records, textbooks, athletic equipment, and furnishings were lost. The cause of the fire was never determined. (NBAHS.)

In April 1926, after the south school fire, voters approved a bond issue for a larger school building to house all elementary and secondary students. An auditorium and a gymnasium were included for both school and community use. In the meantime, students attended classes in empty buildings, the town hall, and churches. The new school building in the above photograph was constructed in time for the 1927–1928 school year. (NBAHS.)

Clad in their traditional orange and black uniforms, North Baltimore's 18-member 1927 football team was photographed along with their coach, Mr. Priest, outside the new school auditorium. The *Weekly Beacon* listed team members as Barrett, Kramp, Judd, Garrison, Stevenson, Thomas, Swartz, Parson, Garman, Leiter, Deter, Reed, Phillips, Bonner, Francisco, Swartz, Blake, and Kelly and reported that each weighed from 120 to 175 pounds. (James R. Kramp.)

North Baltimore's Boy Scout Troop 315, chartered in 1932, posed on the high school auditorium steps in this 1938 photograph. Troop members are, from left to right, (first row) Richard Reddin, Dale Symonds, Joe Lloyd, Dan Reddin, Richard Northrup, Mark Davis, and Howard Aikens; (second row) Tom Lloyd, Lloyd Wetzel, Reldon Freed, Deloy Bland, Henry Archer, Jack Halboth, Allen Bechtel Jr., and Wilbur Wirt Jr.; (third Row) scoutmaster David Wilson, Myron Wyrick, Melville Neilson, George Foltz, William Roberts, Donn Foltz, Ed Crist, and Bill Lloyd. The scouts' uniforms with their long socks and baggy breeches were similar to World War I U.S. Army uniforms. Later, most of these young men served in World War II or the Korean War. In the postwar period, many became local politicians, physicians, lawyers, volunteer firemen, and other leaders of the community. Troop 315 remained an active scout unit in 2008. (NBAHS.)

Five

WORLD WAR II HOME FRONT AND POSTWAR

Among North Baltimore–area World War II servicemen were the five Swartz brothers whose mother, Carrie Swartz, was honored by commissioning a liberty ship in 1942. Pictured at the ceremony in Baltimore are, from left to right, son Oliver and his wife, Ruth; Charles and Carrie Swartz; and a shipyard representative. The other brothers, Howard, Robert, Dwight, and David, were on active duty at the time (NBAHS.)

In the late 1940s photograph above, a post–World War II Memorial Day parade is beginning in the center of North Baltimore. In the photograph below, several local veterans are riding in a jeep in the 1947 Memorial Day Parade. In the years immediately after the war, such ceremonies were heavily attended. The activities began with a parade from city hall on North Main Street and proceeded to Maplewood Cemetery south of town on State Route 18. There, local leaders and clergy presented their remarks and laid wreaths in memory of fallen servicemen. Ceremonies ended with a 21-gun salute by American Legion Post 539. During World War II, 22 North Baltimore–area servicemen died. In later years, one area service member was killed in the Korean War, and eight others lost their lives in the Vietnam War. (NBAHS.)

North Baltimore was at peace when this picture was taken on December 15, 1947, during the season's first heavy snowfall. The town's Christmas decorations added to the holiday atmosphere along South Main Street. The cars parked along the street are mostly 1940s models, but an early 1930s sedan is parked below the streetlight mounted on a cast-iron pole. (Photograph by H. Emerson Boltz, author's collection.)

In this mid-1950s, west-facing view, North Main Street runs from left to right in the center of the picture and intersects with Broadway Street. The late 19th century commercial area of North Main Street was still largely intact. The large First National Bank Building covers the spot of Bassett L. Peters's original store. By 2008, most of these buildings had burned or been razed. (NBAHS.)

Leonard Trout Sr. founded L. L. Trout's Furniture Store in 1900 on the northwest corner of North Main and West Broadway Streets, next to the town hall. Trout's was the largest furniture store in North Baltimore and furnished quality items to many area residents. Leonard Trout Jr. ran the company after his father's death until selling it in 1962. In the c. 1950 photograph below, Len Trout Sr. is seated in front. Behind him are, from left to right, Len Trout Jr., Fran Trout, Mickey McGuire, June Winner, Jorgen Larson, Henry Archer, Barbara Mays, and Tom Kaufman. The building and all its contents were destroyed by fire on January 21, 1971. (Above, Maxine Dulaney Hudson; below, NBAHS.)

The stone-faced building at right was originally built by the Peoples Bank to replace an 1888 building that had burned in 1891. The Peoples Bank operated until 1894 when it closed because the head cashier had embezzled funds. The newly established Hardy Bank took possession of the building in 1896 and remained in business there for 74 years. In 1949, the bank directors modernized the building's exterior (below) by removing the distinctive tower and original entry and adding a new limestone center entrance, which unfortunately destroyed the building's original architectural character. The Peoples Bank and the Hardy Bank were two of four financial institutions established in North Baltimore between 1888 and 1896. The others were the First National Bank and the Home Savings and Loan. All three merged with larger financial institutions in the late 20th century. (Right, NBAHS; below, Maxine Dulaney Hudson.)

On July 31, 1952 at 6:34 a.m., westbound B&O passenger train No. 245 derailed east of North Tarr Street in the middle of North Baltimore. The train was en route from Willard, Ohio, to Garrett, Indiana, and consisted of engine No. 5311, one express car, two baggage cars, one combination baggage-passenger car, and one coach. The train was traveling at 76 miles per hour when it hit a switch that had been incorrectly aligned by the Galatea control tower operator. The locomotive and tender immediately left the track. The engine (above) turned on its side, spun around, and came to rest facing in the opposite direction. The locomotive fireman was killed, and one passenger and six railroad employees were injured. The baggage and passenger cars (below) also derailed but fortunately remained upright or the number of injuries would have been greater. (NBAHS.)

In October 1952, the North Baltimore Fire Department officers and the village mayor proudly posed in front of a newly acquired $15,000 pumper. Pictured are, from left to right, (first row) fireman Harry Kleckner, Mayor Russell Foley, Fire Chief Lee Crouse, and Charles Brumbaugh; (second row) Ed Boney, Mel Patterson, Harry Rogers, and Andrew Lloyd Jr. (NBAHS.)

In this 1948 photograph, North Baltimore Fire Department members have assembled for their annual dinner. For many members, service as a volunteer fireman was a family tradition, sometimes spanning several generations. In Fire Chief Crouse's family, both his son William Clair Crouse and grandson William Lee Crouse were firefighters. Other firemen spent decades with the department such as Harry Kleckner, who served for over 50 years before retiring. (NBAHS.)

The Columbia Hotel, 117–121 North Main Street, went out of business in the early 1930s. Ernie Walters subsequently purchased the building, converting it for multiple uses. In this 1950 view, the old Columbia Hotel Building street level is occupied by the Virginia Theater and Overmier's Rexall Drug Store, while Red's Restaurant is on the second floor. The Walters family lived on the third floor. (Maxine Dulaney Hudson.)

In August 1950, Ralph "Red" Wolfe and his wife, Mary, rented the Miller building at 100 North Main Street, refurbished the interior, and opened the M&R Restaurant. The initials, M&R, represented the first letters of the owners' names. Newlove's Restaurant had gone out of business there after fire damaged the interior. Emil Miller, owner of the building, had a restaurant at that address in 1905. (NBAHS.)

M & R

Meals with Pop or Milk 5c Extra

ROAST CHICKEN
(Potatoes, Two Side Dishes, Bread and Butter, Drink) $1.25

SWISS STEAK
(Potatoes, Two Side Dishes, Bread and Butter, Drink) $1.25

BAKED HAM
(Potatoes, Two Side Dishes, Bread and Butter, Drink) $1.25

ROAST BEEF
(Potatoes, ONE Side Dishes, Bread and Butter, Drink) $1.25

COLD HAM and POTATO SALAD
(Two Side Dishes, Bread and Butter, Drink) $1.25

VEGETABLE PLATE
(Four Side Dishes, Bread and Butter, Drink) ....90¢

BREADED VEAL
(Potatoes, Two Side Dishes, Bread and Butter, Drink) $1.25

RIB-EYE STEAK (6oz.)
(Potatoes, Two Side Dishes, Bread and Butter, Drink) $1.35

SIRLOIN STEAK (8oz.)
(Potatoes, One Side Dish, Bread and Butter, Drink) $1.60

MUSHROOM STEAK
(Potatoes, Two Side Dishes, Bread and Butter, Drink) $1.35

FRIED HAM
(Potatoes, Two Side Dishes, Bread and Butter, Drink) $1.25

TWO GRILLED PORK CHOPS
(Potatoes, One Side Dish, Bread and Butter, Drink) $1.35

BERMUDA GRILLED STEAK
(Potatoes, TWO Side Dish, Bread and Butter, Drink) $1.35

CLUB STEAK (Fried to Your Taste)
(Potatoes, One Side Dish, Bread and Butter, Drink) $1.75

FRIED HAM STEAK
(Potatoes, One Side Dish, Bread and Butter, Drink) $1.50

T-BONE STEAK (Fried to Your Taste)
(Potatoes, One Side Dish, Bread and Butter, Drink) $2.25

HAMBURGER STEAK
(Potatoes, Two Side Dishes, Bread and Butter, Drink) $1.25

21 SHRIMP-IN-A-BASKET
Side Dishes Extra .... 99¢

SHRIMP DINNER (Four Large Shrimp)
(Potatoes, Two Side Dishes, Bread and Butter, Drink) $1.35

FISH FILLET
(Potatoes, Two Side Dishes, Bread and Butter, Drink) $1.25

FRIED OYSTERS (Four Large Oysters)
(Potatoes, Two Side Dishes, Bread and Butter, Drink) $1.50

FRIED HALF-CHICKEN (Disjointed and Breaded)
(Potatoes, One Side Dish, Bread and Butter, Drink) $1.50

CHICKEN LEG and THIGH
(Potatoes, Two Side Dishes, Bread and Butter, Drink) $1.25

The T-bone steak dinner for $2.25 is the most expensive item on this early 1950s M&R Restaurant menu. This restaurant, at 100 North Main Street, was a popular spot throughout the day for local businessmen, workers, teenagers, and families. It was not uncommon to see a B&O locomotive parked on the railroad spur next to the restaurant during the noon hour, with the crew inside having lunch. Teenagers frequently stopped at the M&R Restaurant for a late night snack and to socialize with their friends after a high school football or basketball game. Their tastes usually ran more toward hamburgers and milk shakes than the full course meals on this menu. The owners, Red and his wife, Mary, sold the business in 1961, but a restaurant occupied the building until it burned in February 1981. Red also operated Red's Restaurant, at 119½ North Main Street, above the Virginia Theatre, from 1943 until 1952. This facility served as the meeting location for Rotary and Lions as well as for other clubs and private parties. (NBAHS.)

When compared with the c. 1900 photograph on page 30, this 1950s view of the commercial area of Main Street shows many changes. Although the basic buildings are the same, by 1950, owners had begun modernizing facades and store entrances, efforts that destroyed many of the 19th century features. Ornate architectural pinnacles, other roof line decorations, and balconies with decorative iron railings had been removed. Commercial advertising signs in 1950 included multicolored neon lights that glowed brightly at night. Streetcar tracks had been taken out, and the brick street surface had been covered by asphalt, which was considered cheaper to maintain. In 1950, the roadway remained wide, a feature that had allowed a team of horses to make a legal U-turn in 1900 but which was illegal for automobiles in 1950. Perhaps the most positive change was the replacement of sidewalk utility poles and lines with cast iron light poles. (Maxine Dulaney Hudson.)

After retiring from the grocery business, John Deter ran a small convenience store on West Broadway Street from the 1940s until the late 1950s. John and his wife, Sophronia, sold gasoline from the single pump outside and a limited variety of mostly food items inside. In particular, Deter's was a favorite source of penny candy, soft drinks, and other treats for local school children. (NBAHS.)

Another source of cold refreshment on summer days in the early 1950s was the Foamy Mug, located on North Baltimore's west side at West State Street and Mitchell Road. It primarily served root beer and ice cream and was popular with teenagers and families. The Foamy Mug was built by Stanley and Alma Woessner and Geraldine and Joe Sterling and operated until the mid-1950s. (Beverly Woessner Straley.)

In 1947, the local amateur baseball team, the North Baltimore Canners, won 9 and lost 13 games. Team members pictured are, from left to right, (first row) Ed Hartigan, Ross Shawaker, Clair Blackall, Carl Mumy, Don Boney, Gene Savieo, and Harold Moore; (second row) Dean Conine, Ralph Cook, Bernard Lombard, Don Hampshire, Tom Atkin, Ross Stockwell, Al Ebright, and Bruce Sidebottom. Tom Boltz is the young boy seated in front. (NBAHS.)

Wixom Quarry, approximately one mile north of North Baltimore, was mined in the early 1900s but filled with water after being abandoned. In the 1930s, local groups developed the quarry for swimming, but vandalism forced its closure in 1940. In the 1950s, community members organized Wixom Sports Incorporated and reopened the quarry for swimming. The site continued in operation until the 1970s when financial and volunteer support waned. (NBAHS.)

Six

CYGNET, JERRY CITY, AND GALATEA

The oil boom was responsible for Cygnet's establishment in 1889. In this 1908 picture collage are, from left to right, (top row) the Catholic, Disciples of Christ, and United Brethren churches; (middle row) railroad depot, public school, and Methodist Church; (bottom row) Front Street looking west, Front Street looking east, and a bird's-eye view from atop an oil derrick. (Maxine Dulaney Hudson.)

Toledo, Columbus & Cincinnati R R

SOUTH BOUND.			Stations.	NORTH BOUND.		
Ex—Ex.—Ex.—				Ex.	Ex.	Ex·
A. M.	A M.	P. M.		A. M	P. M	P. M.
7 00	10 30	4 30	ʟ. Toledo ᴀ ʀ	9 00	3 35	6 40
7 05	10 35	4 36	Yondota st	8 54	3 28	6 35
7 15	10 42	4 42	Prentice	8 48	3 22	6 30
7 22	10 49	4 48	Oregon Rd.	8 42	3 15	6 24
7 31	10 58	4 57	Lime City	8 33	3 06	6 15
7 41	11 07	5 07	Dowling	8 22	2 55	6 05
7 44	11 10	5 10	Dunbridge	8 18	2 51	6 01
7 49	11 14	5 15	Sugar R.	8 15	2 46	5 56
7 53	11 18	5 19	Newtons	8 08	2 42	5 51
8 02	11 25	5 26	B. Green	8 04	2 38	5 47
8 10	11 33	5 36	Portage	7 56	2 27	5 36
8 16	11 39	5 41	Mermill	7 50	2 21	5 29
8 22	11 45	5 47	Mungen	7 43	2 15	5 23
8 25	11 48	5 50	Trombley	7 40	2 12	5 20
8 28	11 52	5 53	Cygnet	7 37	2 09	5 17
8 33	11 58	5 58	Oil Center	7 31	2 03	5 12
8 40	12 05	6 06	**Welker**	7 24	1 57	5 05
8 46	12 11	6 12	Van Buren	7 17	1 50	4 57
8 52	12 17	6 18	Stewartsv'e	7 11	1 45	4 50
9 08	12 35	6 32	N. Findlay	6 57	1 32	4 37
9 10	12 35	6 35	ᴀ Findlay ʟ	6 55	1 30	4 35
A. M.	A M.	P. M.		A. M.	P. M.	P. M.

This 1889 Toledo, Columbus, and Cincinnati Railroad train schedule lists three passenger trains a day in each direction stopping in Cygnet. Local passenger trains like these were slow because they stopped briefly at every station, but they were also the cheapest form of railroad travel. There were 14 scheduled stops between downtown Toledo and Cygnet, and a one-way trip took at least 90 minutes. Travelers connected with the B&O at the town of Welker (later renamed Galatea) to the south. This railroad line, which after 1883 linked Cygnet to Toledo to the north and Findlay to the south, was an important factor in Cygnet's rapid development into a supply center for the local oil fields. The railroad allowed shippers to easily bring in large quantities of heavy metal pipes and other materials needed by the oil companies. The town's 3,000 residents were also dependent on railroad shipments for most of their consumer goods. In 2008, the tracks were still in use, but the railroad line had changed ownership many times since the 19th century. (NBAHS.)

By 1903, the Toledo, Bowling Green, and Southern Interurban Streetcar Line provided another option for north or south travel from Cygnet. Interurban cars serving larger communities arrived and departed every two hours, but "locals," which served smaller communities, ran every hour. In this 1905 photograph, passengers are boarding car 135 at the Cygnet Interurban Station. (WCHS.)

In this *c.* 1890 bird's-eye view of Cygnet looking east, Walbridge Avenue is on the left. Most houses were one-floor wood-frame structures, often rapidly constructed for housing oil workers and their families. In addition to the house, most lots had a shed, outhouse, garden, and a wood fence. This photograph appears to have been taken in the late summer or early fall. (WCHS.)

Like other oil boom towns, Cygnet had many oil wells within its village limits despite the unpleasant and often dangerous side effects. In the photograph above, wells have been drilled within a few feet of several homes, and four stationary steam engines are nearby. Since the wells operated 24 hours a day, seven days a week, residents were subjected to constant noise. In addition, smoke from the coal-fired boilers and fumes from the crude oil were unpleasant and a largely unrecognized health risk. Accidents involving fire and explosions were common. When a nitroglycerin wagon exploded during an oil well shooting on September 7, 1897, Cygnet suffered major damage to its commercial area and nearby houses, six people were killed, and many were injured. In the photograph below, spectators are viewing the aftermath of the explosion. (WCHS.)

This early 1900s photograph shows Buckeye Pipeline's Station 8 near Cygnet, which housed massive pumps to service a new large pipeline. Initially rail cars were the primary means of moving oil from large holding tanks to refineries. However, to move oil faster, the Buckeye Pipeline Company constructed an oil pipeline to Chicago in 1888. (Maxine Dulaney Hudson.)

In this c. 1900 winter scene, Cygnet can be seen on the horizon. A prosperous looking farm is in the foreground. Many farmers, who had been living at subsistence level prior to the oil boom, became wealthy by leasing their land to drilling companies. Rents were usually calculated as a fraction, often as high as one-eighth, of the sale price of crude oil produced. (WCHS.)

In the early 1900s photograph above, a man is driving his buggy away from the Cygnet Post Office. The snow is deep and unplowed, and only a few people are walking along Front Street. In the 1913 photograph below, men are poling a makeshift raft down a Cygnet street after heavy rain severely overflowed Rocky Ford Creek. From March 23 to March 27, 1913, Ohio was struck with its greatest natural disaster when the entire state was hit by massive floods. Rainfall of from 6 to 11 inches fell over most of the state, including Wood and the other counties of northwestern Ohio. Because the ground was frozen, rainwater did not soak in and instead poured into streams and rivers, flooding many local areas. (WCHS.)

In the 1907 photograph above, Chester Clark, standing, and Harry Hudson, sitting, are on the front landing of Frank Loes' Grocery store on Front Street in Cygnet. The two-story, wood-frame, false-front building is typical of those erected by entrepreneurs who needed a cheap building fast. A garden seed box is displayed to the right of the door, and a galvanized washtub is hanging on the roof support post. In the photograph below, two young boys are carrying flour sacks, while a third is holding a cardboard food container. Standing behind them is store clerk Harry Hudson. By the early 1900s, prepackaged food like this was becoming common because customers felt it was of higher quality and more sanitary than food scooped from large barrels by the grocer. (Maxine Dulaney Hudson.)

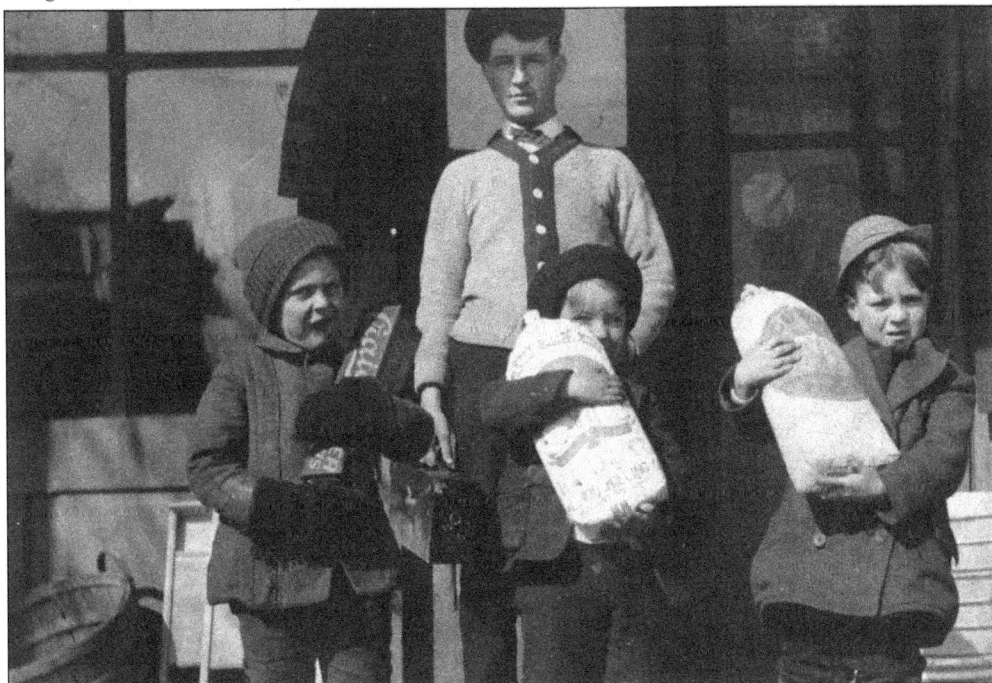

In this early 1900s photograph, future Cygnet businessman Harry Hudson is standing beside a horse-drawn grocery delivery wagon. Horses were the most common mode of local transportation, and runaways were a frequent problem. Reportedly Hudson was nearly killed one Sunday on his way to his girlfriend's home when his horse was "spooked" and suddenly ran away with his rig. (Maxine Dulaney Hudson.)

This 1908 photograph shows the old Cygnet school. The Cygnet School District was created in April 1895 by the Bloom Township Trustees. The first school was a one-room building used for multiple grades. As the village grew, the town added classrooms and eventually erected the school in this photograph, which was located at the north end of Venango Street. (Maxine Dulaney Hudson.)

After the oil boom, Cygnet became a sleepy rural village that supported a variety of small merchants and a single bank. These stores sold a limited variety of quick-turnover groceries and other products in order to make a profit. George C. Searfoss, who operated a small grocery store from 1951 to 1958 on Front Street, was a typical Cygnet businessman. Searfoss also sold gasoline from a small pump outside the store. It was customary in the 1950s for a store employee to pump the customer's gas and wash the car windows. In the 1955 picture below, Searfoss is talking to an unidentified female customer while his son Ken mans the pump. In the late 1950s, many small store owners began to close because they could not compete with the larger stores in Bowling Green or Toledo. (Ken Searfoss.)

The Cygnet fire department's two fire engines can be seen in this 1959 photograph of the combination city hall and fire station. After major portions of Cygnet's mostly wood-frame business district burned in 1891, the village organized a fire department in 1892. After a second fire in 1894, local merchants rebuilt many of the lost structures with brick. Some of these brick buildings were still in use in 2008. (WCHS.)

This 1960 aerial photograph looks northwest across much of Cygnet. Front Street is in the lower foreground. A long train of empty coal cars is headed south past the depot on the New York Central Railroad line (previously the Toledo and Ohio Central) in the left background. Tree-lined Rocky Ford Creek flows from the southwest and converges with the railroad at the top right of the picture. (WCHS.)

Incorporated in 1875, Jerry City followed the boomtown pattern of rapid population growth then decline as the oil wells ran dry. The Toledo, Bowling Green, and Southern Interurban Line built a spur into Jerry City from Trombley on the mainline in 1903 over which it operated a very small streetcar, locally nicknamed the "Dinky." Passengers could transfer to the main interurban line at Trombley. (WCHS.)

This *c.* 1900 photograph shows the interior of Martin Seward's Jerry City butcher shop. Unrefrigerated meat is hanging from hooks on the left wall, while sausage links are displayed behind an open cooler cabinet door in the right background. While food handling regulation and inspection were subjects of much medical and political debate, few regulations had yet been imposed. (WCHS.)

In this early 1900s photograph, a B&O train has stopped to pick up passengers at the Galatea depot. In the steam clouds, the fireman can be seen checking the engine's driving rods and wheel axle journal boxes for needed maintenance. This depot and its freight house constituted a major transfer point at the intersection of the east-west running B&O main line between Chicago and Baltimore and the north-south running Toledo and Ohio Central Railway line. Passengers would detrain here to await a connection, and cargo would be unloaded for transfer. Chesapeake Bay Oysters would arrive by the barrel from Baltimore shippers and be sent north to Toledo and Detroit. Tobacco products from Maryland and Virginia were another frequent transshipment. The Galatea station was torn down in the mid-1930s. The B&O interlocking tower is in the right background. (Bonnie Knaggs.)

The Galatea B&O interlocking tower controlled the switches for both the B&O mainline and the Toledo and Ohio Central Railway (later New York Central) tracks from the 1890s until the late 1960s. The tower operator used a series of levers to move the track switches. He had to pay close attention to all train movements, telegraph messages, signal lights, and operating procedures. (Iris Sewell Holloway.)

The rundown looking hotel in this *c.* 1890 photograph of Galatea served traveling salesmen, oil field workers, and railroad crewmen. Travelers wishing better accommodations could take a dray wagon to North Baltimore. During the oil boom, Galatea, originally known as Welker, had its own saloons, grocery stores, school, hotel, and over 50 houses. (NBAHS.)

The Manhattan Oil Refinery operated in Galatea from 1892 until approximately 1905. It was a large facility located northeast of the B&O and Toledo and Ohio Central Railway junction and employed several hundred men at the height of its operation. The company owned 15 houses for its workers along Eagleville Road between Galatea and North Baltimore, but most lived in other communities. The refinery mainly produced kerosene and shipped it to urban markets using the tank cars seen in the photograph. The railroad cars in the center background probably hauled coal used to heat the crude oil in the refining process. An oil-loading platform stretched along the B&O tracks to the east. The refinery's operations were profitable when John D. Rockefeller's Standard Oil Company purchased it in 1901. However, Rockefeller shut it down to consolidate operations under his monopoly elsewhere. All that remains today are some dry oil patches among trees on the refinery's site. (NBAHS.)

Seven

HOYTVILLE, HAMMANSBURG, AND RUDOLPH

Hoytville's original B&O depot was destroyed in a 1913 train wreck. The replacement building, shown in this photograph, burned in 1965. Incorporated in 1886, Hoytville, Jackson Township's largest community, prospered during the oil boom. In 1927, it still had five grocery stores, four churches, and other services, but it slowly declined over the next 50 years. (Beth Wall Brumbaugh.)

In this photograph, Hoytville residents are preparing to celebrate the Fourth of July in 1911. The Hoytville Bank and other buildings are decorated with banners, and booths are being set up. While Memorial Day was a somber, quiet holiday, the Fourth of July was a time for fun and feasting. (Beth Wall Brumbaugh.)

Francis Wall and his son Howard, who did custom butchering, are shown in front of Wall's Grocery Store on South Main Street in Hoytville in the early 1900s. Another son, Harold, took over operation of the store in 1937. The family resided in part of the building. Village stores were often unofficial social centers where neighbors met and exchanged local news. (Beth Wall Brumbaugh.)

Opening in April 1907, the Hoytville Bank served area farmers and merchants for 24 years. In this c. 1920 photograph, two of the officers are standing in front of the bank building on Hoytville's South Main Street. The advertisement painted on the window notes that the bank was paying four percent interest on deposits left for six months. The bank officers at the time of this photograph were John H. Hanna, president; George F. Dunn Sr. and Joseph Herringshaw, vice presidents; William Hauer, cashier; and George F. Dunn Jr., assistant cashier. Generally bankers were respected community leaders who often served on school and church boards. The Hoytville Bank was forced to close in 1931 because farmers could not make payments on their loans. Crop prices had fallen and land values with them, causing many borrowers to default. Unfortunately the Hoytville bank became insolvent, and the depositors lost their funds. (Beth Wall Brumbaugh.)

In this early 1900s photograph, a man has finished leveling a newly poured sidewalk along Hoytville's West Church Street. His efforts were probably part of a project, begun in 1907, to install one and a half miles of sidewalks throughout the village. The people in the picture may be the homeowner and his family. (Nancy Buchanan.)

In this 1930s photograph, Elijah Dulaney is standing in front of his general store in Hammansburg, one of Henry Township's three surviving oil boom–era communities. During the oil boom, it contained several grocery stores, a blacksmith, stave mill, school, and a church. By the 1930s, only a car dealership, a schoolhouse, a dozen houses, and Dulaney's general store remained. (Maxine Dulaney Hudson.)

The early 1930s photograph above is of Wilson Dulaney's Hudson automobile dealership in Hammansburg. Hudson automobiles were produced from 1909 to 1954 when the company merged with American Motors. Hudsons were noted for their innovative technical designs, including dual brakes, dashboard oil and generator warning lights, and step-down passenger frames. Dulaney operated the Hammansburg dealership until the early 1970s when he ceased selling cars and sold the building. A new owner used the building as an automobile repair garage until closing it in the 1980s. In the lower photograph, Wilson and Belle Northrup Dulaney's daughters, Maxine (left) and Donna Jean (right), pose on Hammansburg Road with their father's car dealership in the right background. (Maxine Dulaney Hudson.)

The *c.* 1900 photograph above provides a view west along Rudolph's Main Street toward the intersection of the north-south Rudolph Road. The large northwest corner building housed the Rudolph Bank and an opera house. On the south side, the first building housed a hardware and oil well supply store. The F. A. Jones Drug Store occupied the southwest corner building. The Cincinnati, Hamilton, and Dayton Railway branch line to North Baltimore ran west of the intersection. The lower photograph shows the vacant 1899 opera house as it looked in the 1950s. Shortly thereafter, it became a U.S. Post Office and remained so in 2008. Rudolph was named after Henry J. Rudolph, a local merchant and postmaster. During the oil boom, Rudolph's population swelled to as many as 1,500 residents but declined after the wells ran dry. (WCHS.)

Eight

RURAL SOUTHERN WOOD COUNTY AND VANISHED VILLAGES

Charles Heath and his family, pictured here, were typical of farmers near Rudolph during the late 1800s and early 1900s. Farmers worked the land despite the oil boom's environmental destruction. Oilmen cared little about the damage caused by gushers and oil spills and moved on when they considered their work done. It was the farmers who were left to clean up and restore the land to productivity. (WCHS.)

This c. 1915 photograph of a Wood County road illustrates the rustic but picturesque condition of much of the area's rural road system in the late 19th and early 20th centuries. The original pioneer road system contained many curved roads leading from one settlement to another. In the 1850s, the county government straightened the roads, aligning them with drainage ditches and used dirt from the ditches to raise the roadbed. Neighboring farmers often provided labor, horses, and equipment as payment for the assessed road improvements. Even with these improvements, travel remained difficult, and horses often sank to their knees in mud during wet weather. By the 1890s, county and township officials had improved many of the roads further by laying gravel from the county's many small quarries on road surfaces. The photograph below shows such work in progress. (WCHS.)

In this *c.* 1900 photograph, a U.S. mail carrier is delivering to a rural Wood County resident. At that time, the Rural Free Delivery program was relatively new, having been implemented in 1896 at the urging of the Grange and other national farm organizations. After that, southern Wood County rural residents had first class mail delivery to their homes almost daily. Parcel Post service for package delivery began in 1913, stimulating a boom in sales to farm families. The popularity of these programs influenced Congress to allocate federal funds in 1916 for improving rural roads. Prior to Rural Free Delivery, rural residents often had difficulty obtaining their mail. People living in Henry Township had to travel to Van Buren in Hancock County until 1874, when the federal government authorized a post office in North Baltimore. During the oil boom, more local post offices opened in hamlets such as Trombley and Galatea, but people still had to travel to a post office to collect their mail. (WCHS.)

In the *c.* 1900 photograph at left, a farmer is holding his two draft horses. Northwest Ohio farmers preferred horses rather than mules to pull their farm machinery and wagons. Most were mixed breeds rather than purebreds. Farmers took pride in their teams, and neighbors generally looked down upon those who mistreated or neglected their animals. In the 1880s photograph below, John Haen, a German immigrant farmer, is plowing his field in northeast Henry Township. Plowing with horses required skill and a well-trained team to keep the rows straight. The plowshare had to be kept smooth, clean, and rust free in order to smoothly move through the soil. Draft horses were present on every farm until they were largely replaced by tractors by the late 1930s. (Left, Maxine Dulaney Hudson; below, Millie Kramp Broka.)

A major crop for most 19th and early 20th century Wood County farmers was wheat, which, after the 1860s, was harvested using a thresher that separated the seed from the chaff. In the picture above, two threshing machines are at work, each powered by a steam traction engine. One thresher owner usually served many wheat farms in a geographic region, traveling from farm to farm and depending on area farmers to cooperatively assist in each other's threshing operations. Individual farmers prepared their grain bins and sacks, arranged for the threshing machine to arrive at a specified time, and cut and gathered their wheat into sheaves in the field. On threshing day, neighboring farmers convened at the designated farm for what was to be a hard day's work. The photograph below provides a closer view of a steam traction engine. (WCHS.)

In this photograph, a crew stands in front of a thresher and steam engine. Threshing was a labor-intensive operation, which required several dozen men to complete each farm's harvest in one day and, thus, avoid bad weather. The thresher owner and his helper assembled and maintained the equipment, fired the steam engine boiler, and maintained steam pressure. Neighboring farmers manned horse-drawn wagons that brought in the sheaves, fed sheaves into the thresher, filled the grain sacks, and carried the sacks to grain bins. The dirtiest and hottest job was standing atop the straw pile distributing the straw evenly as it was blown out of the thresher. The farmer whose grain was being threshed usually did that job. The farmer's wife typically took pride in preparing a good meal for the workers. Food preparations began a day or two ahead, and the women were up early on threshing day to have a meal ready by noon. Aided by daughters and neighboring women, each farm wife was expected to provide a large quantity and variety of dishes. (NBAHS.)

This c. 1900 picture of a steam traction engine and crew was taken in Hoytville at the intersection of Church and Main Streets. The traction engine belonged to Robert W. C. Buchanan, who is seated just behind the big road wheel. In addition to powering threshers, steam tractors were used to run portable sawmills and for hauling heavy cargos. But transporting and using them was hard and dangerous work. The engine's heavy weight and the poor condition of the dirt roads limited their use to times when the roads were dry or frozen so that they would not sink into the mud. Operators were occasionally killed or injured when the heavy engines broke through poorly supported bridges or when improperly maintained boilers exploded. By 1940, gasoline-engine tractors pulling newly developed combines had replaced steam traction engines and threshing machines for grain harvesting throughout Wood County. Most farmers owned their own combines, and one or two men could harvest an entire farm on their own, freeing them from dependence on their neighbors for labor. (Nancy Buchanan.)

The Boozers were a farm family who lived near Cygnet in Bloom Township from the 1870s until the early 1900s. In this c. 1900 picture, Mary Jane Boozer is preparing to milk what appears to be a Brown Swiss, a popular milk-cow breed. Since cows had to be milked twice a day, the number owned was directly related to the number of family members capable of milking. Farm children were taught to milk as soon as they were old and strong enough. Available pastureland was also a limiting factor. Farmers sold their milk to local creameries, which then processed the raw milk into dairy products for retail sale. In the 1950s, when the state government issued stronger dairy sanitation regulations, most southern Wood County farmers gave up the milk business rather than bear the expense of purchasing new equipment. (WCHS.)

In this c. 1915 photograph, Hoytville butcher Howard Wall, aided by a Jackson Township farmer, is butchering a hog. In the 19th and early 20th centuries, farmers usually sold most of their livestock but butchered some for their own family. Often helped by a neighbor, the men did most of the work outdoors in the winter. After killing the hog and removing its internal organs, which were saved, the carcass was dipped in a huge kettle of boiling water to remove the hair. After skinning, the meat was cut into pieces and taken to the house where the women prepared it for canning, sausage, or smoking. Nothing was wasted, with the intestines used for sausage casings, the fat made into lard, and everything else processed but the "squeal." Some farmers were noted locally for their quality smoked meats and had private customers in the neighboring towns. (Beth Wall Brumbaugh.)

WILLIAM F. STEIFF WHOLESALE MEATS. NO. BALTIMORE. OHIO   C-4

This *c.* 1940 photograph is an aerial view of the William F. Steiff Wholesale Meat Company, which was located on Hough Road approximately a mile west of North Baltimore. Local farmers increased their cash income by selling livestock to local wholesale butchers whose market was regional rather than local. Steiff primarily bought steers and hogs from local farmers and then butchered them at this facility. Steiff was able to process many animals in a day using hired workers who performed specialized tasks. Companies like his sold their products to groceries and meat markets in the larger towns and cities in northwest Ohio. Steiff ceased operations in 1941 after a fire of undetermined origin destroyed most of his buildings. A remaining building was converted to a house and later, after being painted in psychedelic designs, was a notorious site of rock concerts. The building was razed in the 1970s. (NBAHS.)

Most farm families kept chickens both for their own consumption and for sale. In this c. 1925 photograph, Claude and Marian Brobst's daughter Jeanne is feeding chickens on her parents' Oil Center Road farm. Feeding and watering a large chicken flock was labor intensive. Eggs were gathered daily for sale either to local stores or individual customers, and hens required special attention and housing when brooding. (Author's collection.)

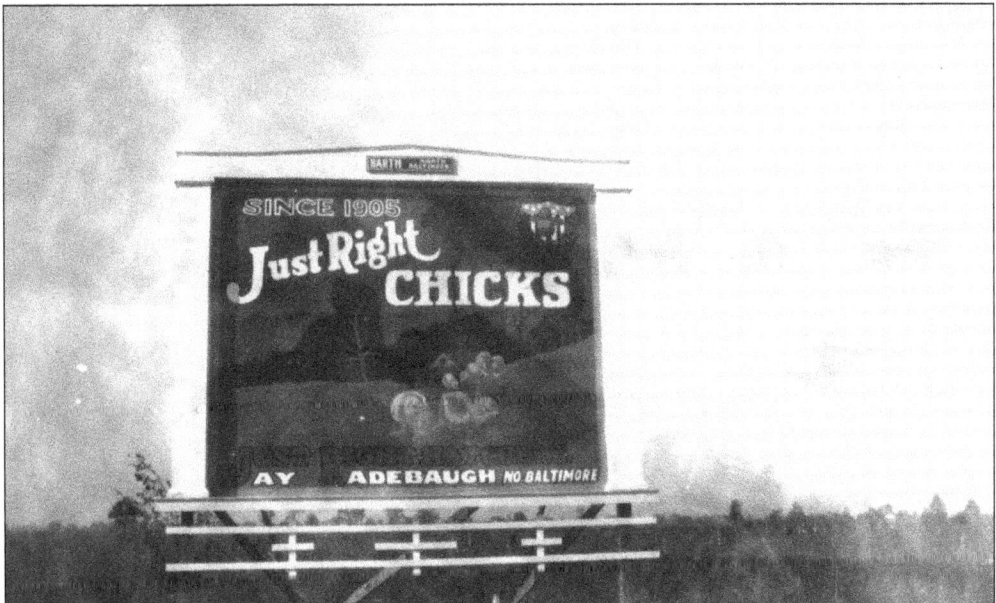

Local hatcheries made a farmer's life easier by hatching the eggs in incubators and then selling the young chicks. North Baltimore's Just Right Hatchery, whose advertisement is shown in this photograph, was in business from 1907 until the early 1950s. Jay Radabaugh operated the hatchery at 303 West Maple Street. After 1950, most Wood County farmers stopped raising chickens due to low prices and competition from large-scale chicken farms. (WCHS.)

Most rural southern Wood County residents did not have electric power before the Hancock-Wood Electric Co-op was organized in 1938 as part of the federal government's rural electrification efforts. The co-op's field crews and their trucks are shown in this c. 1940 photograph taken outside its 118 South Main Street headquarters in North Baltimore. Standing are, from left to right, ? Sterling, Dowling Hamman, Alvin Baher, Bob Roth, Harold Richmond, A. J. Phillips, Harold Dick, George Gillon, Frank Dick, Pete Sprague, Sylvester Herr, Clell Flowers, and R. Powers Luse, general manager. North Baltimore had an electric power plant by the early 1890s, but it did not serve the rural community because, like most private power companies, its owners felt it was not cost effective to build electric lines throughout the countryside. In southern Wood County, a few farms located near the interurban streetcar lines were allowed to tap the streetcar's power cables, but most farm families used kerosene lamps for lighting. (Hancock-Wood Electric Co-op.)

Hancock-Wood's main office was established in North Baltimore because the town was centrally located in the co-op's service area. By the mid-1930s, a majority in congress supported rural electrification, and a series of court cases enabled the federal government to become involved. In 1935, Pres. Franklin Roosevelt signed into law the Rural Electrification Program that established over 417 electric cooperatives to bring power to agricultural areas. The Wood County–area project originally called for a co-op involving Seneca and Wyandot counties as well as Hancock and Wood, but it was decided to split off the two western counties and create a separate organization. In 1938, the Hancock-Wood Electric Co-op was organized, and in March 1939 it began to build power lines throughout Wood and Hancock Counties. In this photograph, from left to right, Jim Smith, Alvin Baher, and an unidentified crew member are preparing to install a pole along a county road. Much of the work was done by hand. (Hancock-Wood Electric Co-op.)

After the Hancock-Wood Co-op was organized, its field crews, along with some contractors, began to erect power distribution lines along rural roads as rapidly as possible. In the late 1930s, the large private power companies such as Toledo Edison and Ohio Power reversed their previous positions and decided to expand into rural areas and compete with the new cooperatives. However, many rural residents favored the co-op and urged Hancock-Wood crews to build their lines as fast as possible before one of the big companies could move in. In one case, a farm wife physically embraced a newly erected Ohio Power pole to prevent the line from being built, thus saving her neighborhood for the co-op. Since the company began serving customers in 1939, its field crews have continued to construct new transmission lines, upgrade existing lines, and repair storm damage. In this c. 1960 photograph, from left to right, linemen Ray Jameson, Phillip Vandersool, and George Gillen are working on a pole high above the flat Wood County countryside. (Hancock-Wood Electric Co-op.)

This August 8, 1939, photograph commemorates the first electric meter installation on the Ober Apple farm at 16792 State Route 18 in Henry Township. From left to right are field crew members Emery Jimison Jr. and R. M. "Pert" Hindall; Mrs. Ober Apple, homeowner; and C. C. Doyle, Hancock-Wood Electric Co-op general manager. By the end of 1939, the co-op had over 870 customers, and by December 1941, it had wired over 2,000 rural homes for electricity. In addition, special programs helped rural residents purchase their first electric appliances such as cooking ranges from local merchants. Once rural areas were electrified, it was found that farmers used more power than city dwellers, thus justifying the initial expense of stringing the distribution lines. Rural electrification was a real boon to Southern Wood County farmers and dramatically changed and improved their standard of living. Rural electrification was one of the most successful of New Deal programs, and the Hancock-Wood Electric Co-op has continued to serve the area's rural residents with over 13,000 customers in 2008. (Hancock-Wood Electric Co-op.)

Located so that no student had to walk more than two miles to attend school, one-room schools were the primary source of education for Wood County's rural elementary students until the early 20th century. In the 1910 photograph above, teacher Ray Coulter and his students are posing in front of the Pedro School at the corner of Oil Center and Potter Roads. The photograph below was taken at the same school in October 1913. Students are, from left to right, (first row) Murl Karian, Frank Vandersall, Kenneth Judd, Wade Loe, Carl Vandersall, Frank George, and Eugene Metz; (second row) Edna Zimmerman, Thelma Apple, Martha Metz, Chloe Delle Foltz, Mana Bland, Faye Bland, and Huldah Zimmerman; (third row) Lulu Hock (teacher), Jake Nier, Earl Rader, Charles George, Wade Vandersall, Otis Rader, Howard Vandersall, Rose Karian, and Mary Zimmerman; (fourth row) Lemuel Rader, ? Dick, Ralph Karian, Herman Hess, Virgil George, and William Hess. (NBAHS.)

West Creek School, located at the intersection of Reigle and Roundhead Roads, was the most southwesterly school in Jackson Township. The township supported approximately nine one-room schools by the early 1900s. In this c. 1900 photograph, West Creek School students are holding shovels and a bucket, possibly having planted a tree or flowers in an Arbor Day celebration. (Nancy Buchanan.)

Located on the corner of Freyman and Rudolph Road, Freyman School's interior was typical of one-room schools in 1905. Students were grouped by grade level, sitting on cast iron and wooden seats aligned in rows in front of the teacher's desk and blackboard. Heating came from a coal-fired stove. (NBAHS.)

1894,- -1895.

OUR SCHOOL.

Sub District No. 3,

Jackson Township, Wood Co., O.

A. D. BUTLER, - - TEACHER.

"LET YOUR LIFE BE LIKE A SNOW FLAKE, WHICH LEAVES A MARK, BUT NOT A STAIN"

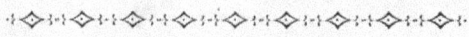

Esther Anderson, Nettie Anderson, Grace Browneller, Earl Browneller,

Maud Burgoon, Lillie Burgoon, Stella Burgoon, Eva Bowden, Coney Bowden, Oney Bowden, Winfield Ferguson, Clark Ferguson,

John Ferguson, Vern Ferguson, Ern Ferguson, Leon Garwood, Clara Garwood, Lulie Garwood, Blanche Gault, Harley Gault,

Ralph Gault, Grace Hackett,

Charlie Hartman, Ira Hoot,

Orlando Hartman, Aaron Hoot,

Pearl Hartman, Wilbur Leather,

Ettie Harter, John Mills,

Stella Harter, Mary Mills,

John Mitchell, Walis Mapes, Scott Mapes, Rena Otto, Rol Otto, Park Otto, Eddie Rhoad, Stella Rhoad, Rose Rhoad, Val Rhoad, Clara Richard, Elma Snyder, Bertha Snyder, Harry Snyder, Oscar Sperow, Delos Sperow, Adam Teatsorth, Roy Teatsorth, Cordie Wilson, Flossie Weaver.

This 1894–1895 school year commemorative card for Jackson Township's sub-district No. 3, lists 52 students, many from the same families. This school was also known as the Dog Town School. A district supervisor administered the school district and made unannounced visits to each school on a regular basis. The local township trustees paid the teachers' salaries, but all textbooks, writing tablets, and other school supplies were purchased by the each pupil's parents. Students could complete the eighth grade, but anyone wishing to go to high school had to enroll in one located in southern Wood County's larger villages. In Ohio, teachers were required to have an eighth grade education and pass the Boxwell examination, a qualification test for entering high school. Eventually teachers were required to graduate from a two-year teacher-training school, then known as normal schools. (Nancy Buchanan.)

Beginning in 1920–1921, the one-room schools were closed as motorized school buses made it possible to transport rural Wood County students to centrally located consolidated township schools that offered both elementary and high school–level education. In this c. 1945 photograph, bus driver C. C. Doyle is picking up students along Liberty High Road in a North Baltimore Public Schools Chevrolet school bus. (Beverly Woessner Straley.)

Shown in this early 1950s photograph, the L. Stanley Woessner farm in Henry Township with its wooden barns was a typical southern Wood County farm. In the 1950s and 1960s, northwest Ohio farming changed drastically as most farmers ceased raising livestock and concentrated on growing grain crops. The importance of barns built primarily for storing hay and sheltering livestock declined, and many fell into disrepair. (Beverly Woessner Straley.)

In the c. 1950 photograph above, Stanley Woessner, standing in barn doorway, and his nephew John Woessner Jr., in the foreground, are repairing a mowing machine prior to cutting hay. After cutting and raking the hay into rows in the field, a hay bailer pulled by a tractor was used to gather and mechanically press the hay into bales, which were then deposited on an attached wagon. The whole operation required only two men. The photograph below shows a wagon stacked with bailed hay at the Woessner's barn. Increased mechanization in the 1940s and 1950s allowed farmers to increase the total amount of land they could till. As a result, the number of farmers decreased, and many farmsteads, including the Woessner's farm buildings, were razed by new absentee landowners to increase cultivated acreage. (Beverly Woessner Straley.)

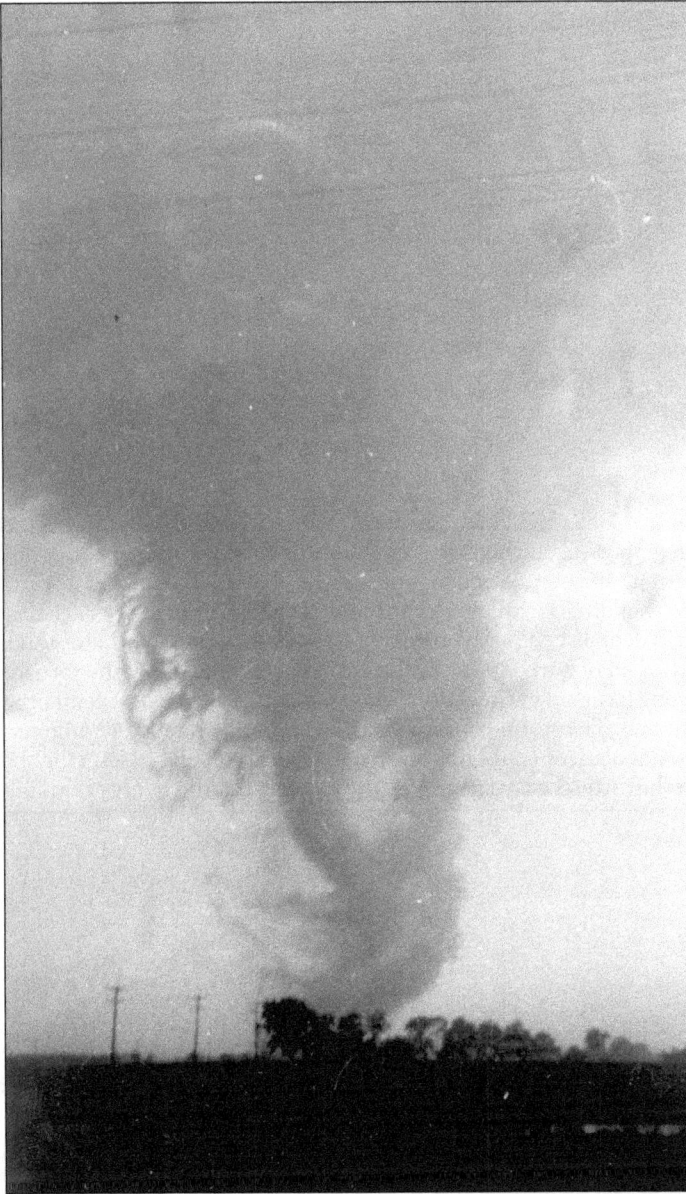

Monday, June 8, 1953, is a day that brought death and destruction to southern Wood County when the area was struck by a major tornado, shown in this photograph. Before this natural disaster was over, the twister had killed nine people, injured many more, and inflicted over a million dollars in property damage. The day began as a typical hot, humid, partly cloudy summer day with a few scattered showers until late afternoon. However, by 6:00 p.m. the entire western sky was covered by a dark storm with a huge thunderhead rising above it moving rapidly from southwest to northeast. At some point, the storm spawned this large tornado that first touched down near Deshler in Henry County but soon crossed into Jackson Township in Wood County. The approximately 300-foot-wide tornado struck a farmhouse killing a mother and her four children while the father watched in horror from a distance. The clear sky and setting sun in the west backlit the tornado in brilliant red as the storm with its tailing funnel cloud continued into Henry Township. (NBAHS.)

These two photographs taken the day after the tornado strike illustrate the devastation found in the storm's path in southern Wood County. In the above aerial view of a destroyed farmstead, only one roofless building is still standing. The photograph below shows the wreckage of a barn and corncrib demolished by the tornado. Remarkably, milk cans are standing, apparently untouched, on the bed of a truck next to the barn. Large trees hit by the tornado were snapped or uprooted. At one farm, an entire dairy herd was destroyed, and, at several others, all the farm buildings were ruined. The storm continued northeastward for about 40 miles until it dissipated over Lake Erie. Ambulances could not meet the need. In several cases, neighbors used pickup trucks and makeshift stretchers to transport the severely injured to area hospitals. (NBAHS.)

Main St. Bays, O.

This *c.* 1900 view of the oil boom hamlet of Bays looks west along Main Street's business block. The small board sidewalk on the right ran three miles west to Wingston and kept the oil field workers and their families out of the mud when traveling to their homes or jobs. Located at the Rudolph and Bays Road junction in Liberty Township, in the 1890s, the town had several stores, a barber, two doctors, a blacksmith, and a Cincinnati, Hamilton and Dayton Railroad depot with a spur line for freight delivery. Six trains a day stopped to pick up passengers. A major fire destroyed most of the commercial buildings in the early 1900s. The community never had more than several hundred inhabitants and shrank in direct proportion to the oil field's decline. The post office was closed in 1915. In 2008, only a few houses remained where Bays once stood. (Author's collection.)

Bays' school, in the photograph above, was located on the northwest corner of Main Street and Rudolph Road. One of the school's two buildings housed grades 1 through 6, while the other contained grades 7 through 10. At one time the school had approximately 150 students and offered two years of high school. The buildings escaped the Bays' fire, but were torn down when the school closed after World War I. (WCHS.)

In its heyday, Trombley, previously named Blake, had several saloons, livery stables, a hotel, railroad depot, general store, and post office. The town's several small industries included a stave mill, boiler factory, a small refinery, and a large oil well supply company. Trombley, built on low lying terrain, frequently flooded, and, when the oil field declined, the residents departed. By 1960, the only building left in Trombley was the abandoned house in the photograph above. (WCHS.)

Located in Bloom Township, Oil Center at its height in the 1890s contained a grocery store, several boarding houses, and a livery stable. The abandoned old house in this 1960 photograph was the last Oil Center building standing. The house pictured was typical of an oil worker's home. Often constructed in a single day, such houses were not insulated and contained only four or five rooms. (WCHS.)

This c. 1960 photograph shows a large Victorian-era farmhouse on the George C. Grant farm outside Cygnet. Many farmers built fine houses of this type with oil-lease revenues earned during the oil boom. Others bought additional farmland, improved their existing farms, or invested in other businesses. Some original landowners' descendents still own their family homesteads, but in 2008, much of Wood County's farmland belonged to absentee landowners. (WCHS.)

As late as the 1960s, physical remnants of the oil boom were still widely evident throughout southern Wood County, and in 2008, one could still find an old oil tank or well head. However, structures like the wooden pump house in the 1960s photograph to the left have mostly disappeared due to the effects of weather and because they were removed as obstacles to farming. Reportedly in 2008, a rusty old boiler like the one in the c. 1950 picture below could still be found along the edge of a local field. The environmental damage caused by gushers and leaking oil tanks has long been eradicated, and the soil returned to productivity. Of concern in 2008, for both safety and environmental reasons, were the occasional crude oil and natural gas leaks from old, poorly capped wells. (WCHS.)

This c. 1950 aerial photograph of North Baltimore was taken facing west. The B&O railroad is the straight line running through the picture's center. The local grain elevator is the tall structure in the left center, and Main Street is the second street west of that structure lined by large commercial buildings. Ohio Route 18 runs along South Main Street through the town then turns west just south of the railroad. The road continues westward toward Hoytville on the far horizon. Between 1900 and 1960, North Baltimore remained this size; between 1960 and 2000, growth was minimal. However, in 2008 the CSX Railroad purchased over 500 acres between Route 18 and the railroad tracks stretching from North Baltimore to Hoytville for an intermodal rail yard. If the facility is built as planned and growth predictions are realized, much of the farmland shown here will be covered with warehouses and other businesses, significantly changing the area. The oil boom's prosperity is only a memory, but a new period of growth for southern Wood County may be on the horizon. (NBAHS.)

Visit us at
arcadiapublishing.com